"OVERCOME" WORDS FOR US

"OVERCOME" Words for YOU

WORDS
O
V
E
FOR
R
C
YOU
O
M

By Bruce Etheridge

OVERCOME

Words for You

"OVERCOME" Words for YOU

"I talked to God the other day…
I thanked him for my Mother…
Then I thanked him for giving me my greatest gift before I was born."

Bruce Etheridge

Dedication Page

I dedicate this book to my loving family, especially my wonderful Mom who has been the fuel of my life, and my Grandmother who happened to be the greatest person I ever met. As it should be my Mother and Grandmother's influence on my life saved me. I also acknowledge my wonderful Wife, who herself was slapped in the face by tragedy years ago but refused to let go of the rope; she survived, revived, and continued to thrive.

These ladies are my testimonies
And ultimate proof that

"Tragedy can be the birth of Greatness"

I also dedicate this book to those in my life that was lost too early. This book would not have been possible without all of you.

Copyright 2015 © by Bruce Etheridge

"OVERCOME" Words for YOU

Birth order should never be taken for granted. My older brother had to experience life in real time, the first time. I was lucky enough to watch and learn from his successes and his mistakes. When you're the oldest, you are going to be insecure at times, unsure of your direction at times, and nervous about expectations at times.

There are many youngsters out there today yearning for the missing piece in their life. I tell you today that the "missing piece is overrated. What you need is a "listening piece. My oldest brother didn't lack for a missing piece, he had that. He just needed a "listening piece". For those of you out there searching to find the missing parent or missing piece…You may find it easier to find a "listening piece".

"If you have a Missing Man in your life, then replace him with a Listening Man"…
"If you have a Missing Piece, then replace it with a Listening Piece"…

His role in my life was important. I believe that I took it for granted during his wonderful 49 years on earth. But once he was gone, I realize the man he was, the man he became, and the man he nurtured me to become.

"I saw what he wanted most in life, and then he taught me that I didn't need it. I saw what he hungered for, and then he convinced me that I was full. I saw him search for completeness, and then he convinced me that I was whole".

If you happen to be younger than the oldest sibling, accept them without judgment, love them unconditionally, and support them without checking the fuel gage. Give abundantly without hesitation. I dedicate this book to my oldest brother who happens to be my greatest teacher along with my Mother. This book would not have been possible without him. Thank you, thank you, and thank you.

"In the end "the struggle" will not win. I look forward to laughing with you again"

Joel Darnell Kindred…My Brother…
My inspiration …

"Don't allow anyone's weakness to get in the way of your responsibility to teach them their Greatness"

"OVERCOME" Words for YOU

Table of Contents

Dedication Page–5
Forward...10
Test Day...14
Legacy Cry / I Believe...16

Table of Contents...8
Words for Who?...11
The Worst Feeling...15
History-(Cover)...17

A VOICE FROM TEMPLE, TX....18

Teaching Quote...24
Teaching Greatness...31
Mr. Z's, Mr. T's, Mr. N's...34
Mr. E's Quotes-...42-47
Shut up & Get Busy-50, 64, 86
"Complete the Man"...54
Mr. E's Quotes...61-89
Greatness Remembered...67
I'm a Hero...70
What does a Hero Look Like-72
My Mother's Family...79
His Smile...82
"The Bully"...92
Growing Periods...100
"Death Bed"...103
Fourth and Inches...112
Imperfect but Perfect"...122
"The Stop Sign"...128
Do You Know CPR?...137
"Forty-three Kicks...139
Mr. E's Words...142-147
Favorite Coach Quote...153
Nearsighted Quote...156
Comments / Reactions...160

The Day My Life Changed"..25
"I'm Not a Statistic"...32
"The Compress"...36
Love Ones left behind...47
Father Needed...52, 83, 145
"Catch That Fly"...56
The Shaded Legacy Tree 62
Attending School...69
Write it Down...71
Man in the Mirror...76
Grandmother-Moment of ...80
Abandonment...85
The Fire...98
The Crossing Tree...102
Mr. E's Words-109-110
Today's Message...119
"Where's my Mom"...125
Serve Purpose Quote...131
"The Wheel Chair"...138
"The Little Voice"...140
"The Punch"...148
A Favorite Quote...155
Message to the Reader...157
Spotlight Writer / Poet...162

WORDS OF ENCOURAGEMENT SPEECHES OF IMPACT...165

Hey Superman...166
Beauty of the Rose...176
Greatness flawed...182

"Let Things Go"...171
"Put the Gun Down-178
Know your Purpose...186

Win the Day…190	What's up, Old Man? …193
Will Never Forget…200	"Chocolate Cake"…202
Responsibility…208	"I Don't Know"…209
"SeaSons Greeting" …211	God has your Back…214
What are you fighting for?-218	Little Empty Today.. 224
"Graduation Day…226	Change for a Change-230
"Respect all Women"…232	The Chair…234
Running for the Answer…238	"Lock Your Faith" …240
Season Angels…242	Racism (Poem)…243
How / Remembered?...245	Insignificant…249, 261
Passion, Not Your Position-250	Respect the Man…252
Farther Needed…253	My Diary…254
You Belong Here…258	What Does a Hero…260
Failure = Success…262	"Race-Time-Choice…265
Ownership…266	Forgive to Live…269

MORE MOTIVATIONAL POEMS (273)

"Dreams and Visions"…272	"Communicate"…275
"The Youngest One"…276	Why today Coach?...278
"Control'…280	My Coach…282
Where's Mom?(spaced)…285	"The Forgetful Man" …286
"This Women"…288	
"Half Full or Half…293	Birth Order/Daddy'sGirl-294
Today's Goal …298	Why am I writing…299
"Thanksgiving Dessert"..300	"I'm A Father Now"…302
"Red Oak Tree"…304	She Motivated Me…306
"A Father's Tough…308	Coaches' Claws…310
"I Am A Man"314	Growing / Document Me…318

"SACRIFICED FOR YOU"…319

"Missing in Action"…320	"Entrenchment"…322
"There He Stood"…324	"Respect the Man…326
"Find the Sparkle"…328	"I like My Nose"…330
"My Anger is Mine"…332	"Magnify Yourself"…333
We Survived…334	Today We Rise-…335
Politics and the Prez…336	Move On…338
Raise your Voice…340	

"REROUTED GLORY"…342

Coaching Excerpts…349	Family Memories…349
My Grandmother…351	Your Page…350
Mama's Notes…353	

COACH ETHERIDGE'S FINAL MESSAGE…354

Foreword

As his talk came to an end, calm came over the room. The sincerity and honesty were almost too much. As my eyes began to cloud, I couldn't help but admire the power of Bruce's words. As I tried to gain my composure, I took a quick glance around and noticed not a dry eye.

Using real-life struggles and situations to reach others, Bruce's words can be your daily dose of courage and hope. His compilation of writings, quotes and poems serve as a brush to the canvas of life. He paints a picture of inspiration that is uplifting; sure to encourage in spite of hardships and difficulties that occur in daily life. Within these pages, the optimism and positive regard can inspire you to OVERCOME.

Anthony Persyn
friend

Words for You...

If you are a teen, mother, father, grandmother, or family...
THIS BOOK IS FOR YOU...
If you are someone caught in "the struggle"...
If you need some old fashion inspiration for your situation...
If you are someone searching or has already found God...
If your heart is aching and you need someone to lift you......
If you're struggling with depression, or a tragic lost...
THIS BOOK IS FOR YOU...
If you are struggling to simply find your purpose...
If you are boy or girl, that has a missing man in your life...
If you're a Religious leader seeking extra words to motivate...
If you are a single parent whose child is lost to the streets...
If you are someone needing a vision to becoming a better you
THIS BOOK IS FOR YOU...
If you are worried about what's next or who's next...
If you are a coach or a teacher or youth leader...
If you are reading this or listening to the audio version...
You are about to be blessed because God's purpose being served...
THIS BOOK IS FOR YOU...

Introduction

One of the most important classes that I ever took was a typing class; it gave me the ability and pathway to document my unaltered thoughts.
"Thoughts change lives"

This book was written to help motivate troubled youth or parents. Hopefully it will provide the additional motivation for you to understand and overcome your current situation. The focus is to remind you that your success lies in your future not in your current situation. I've shared additional stories, and briefs from past years.

You may not agree with all that is within, but apply that which is good for you and move forward with your life. This book is not intended to be the cure for all; it only serves as what was an important tool for me to help those I taught. I share this because this is the fuel that continues to guide many that touched me and that I touch, delivered in a personal way.

I began writing after losing my dear brother. My Savior awoke me to start writing. I did as I was commanded. This is the finished product...not perfect, but finished. "Judgment is mine sayeth the Lord". Although losing my brother was a tragedy, his death motivated me help others even more. His life continues, because his influence drove this project... I love you bro..."**Tragedy can be the Birth of Greatness**"

See you on page one,

Bruce Etheridge

If you don't know How to speak or what to say to a person in "The Struggle"

Here are a few motivational stories, quotes and briefs that have been successful for me.

"If the untold story can help others heal. Then, my story must be shared to seal the deal. Sharing is caring. The healing begins today"...

-*Bruce Etheridge*- "<u>Overcome</u>" <u>Words for You</u>

TEST DAY

Today is test day, a day for all to be tested.
With bitter words, and the angers of life
That struggle to be digested

Fear of the unknown will test each and every HEART
Today's test will never determine the one who's really SMART

Your test today, to survive, understand, and determine the KEY
I must know who I am, and not allow the bitterness to change ME

The test of distraction will include ANGER and HATE
Stay in check today, in me the KEY, I must lock my FAITH

Your test today to checkmate who you are
Determination, understanding, and surviving creates a STAR

Tested with death, lunacy, and life's other dirty tricks
The test includes maximum guilt, maximum filth, to maximize the sick

REMEMBER, today is only a test of FAITH that will never LAST
You pass the test by surviving, smiling, and even laughing at your tested PAST.

"The worst feeling I ever had in my life was to see my Mother Cry"

To be raised by a single parent mother has a significant effect on you.

My Mother and Grandmother became my only safe base. They protected my insecurities, they nurtured my confidence and prayed for my safety. Their prayers got me through some trying times. Sometimes, you just got to survive the trying times… My mother did this in the most facinating way.

I can never hold my head down or let go of the rope. She held on because of us…tears…

If you can't make a positive change for yourself, then you should be able to make a positive change for someone you love and respect. For me it was my Mom and Grandmother. I stayed out of trouble because the fear of breaking their heart. They had already endured enough struggle, pain, and hurt. To see them hurt or cry was just unbearable for me as a teenager and still today…

"I would rather die than see my Mother cry…"

I want my Sons to see me cry for them (my sons)...
I want my Daughter to see me cry for her (my wife)...
Because
I want my Sons to never leave their Sons...
And I want my Daughter to know her value and discover a Man that will value her...

I BELIEVE
Every child born has a purpose in life. The purpose of the child may be yours to fulfill or his to accept. Are you afraid of not fulfilling or serving your purpose?

Someone may be waiting on you to save them. Someone maybe searching for you today, because God has sent them on their purposeful mission to find you hug you, and save you from yourself. You may be someone that's turning a blind eye on your rescuer.

The word INSIGNIFCANT should be removed from the English language.

Everyone Matters... God Bless YOU and enjoy reading.

The History Book Cover

The first time I shared this story with my class was over twenty-four years ago. One of my students was so touched by it that he drew this picture and gave it to me a few days later. He stated that his story was similar to mine. I told him that I would forever hold on to the picture and someday the world would see his work. He smiled, I cried, he hugged me, I held him. He touched my heart, my soul. **"Michael, I hope to find you someday being a great father".** At that moment I realized my story is one that others needed to hear and I needed to share. **"Reveal and Begin to Heal".**

"Nurture their wounds past their shackles"

A Voice From Temple Texas

This is your Life follow your Dreams

I'm the little boy from the Eastside. Temple has hundreds just like me. **You** may be from the Eastside, Westside, Southside or Northside. You may be a youngster playing Pop Warner football: you may play kickball or volleyball at school, or play basketball at the church gyms. You may sing in the choir or play in the Band...you may just attend school and work hard...or you may be one walking the streets, just trying to survive...

You may be a teenager, college student or adult that's going thru the struggle right now: you may have doubts about your direction in life. You may feel overwhelmed with the troubles of today. I'm here today to remind you that your troubles are temporary.

"FAILURE IS THE BIGGEST CONTRIBUTOR TO SUCCESS"

You may have lost someone that you loved very dearly. *"If we forget those that were lost... Then we really lose those we remember"*

You may have doubts about your children, your spouse, and your family. For those of you out there searching to find the missing parent or missing piece…You may find it easier to find a "listening piece".

"If you have a Missing Man in your life, then replace him with a Listening Man"…"If you have a Missing Piece, then replace it with a Listening Piece"…

You may come from imperfect parents; you may come from families that are imperfect. You may be walking the sidewalks the low income housing. Listen to me today…

You are the Truth, You are not a lie.
Your time has come…

We see you and believe in you. Come on, you can make it. So many people care for you. *You must believe that you can make it… Don't give up, don't give in, don't quit. There are heroes looking for you. God is sending heroes to save you to serve their purpose. Position yourself now…Quit hiding behind anger, bitterness and frustration. Allow them to find you, serve you, and fulfill their purpose.*

They are teaching, volunteering, coaching, and mentoring those of you willing to listen. Listen to them. They will not give up on you. <u>*"You are not a victim, you are a product. It's time to produce."*</u>

Obstacles are faced in every city in America. It does not have to be you. Change in you is coming.

Take pride, listen, educate yourself, and hug your Mama or Grandmother or somebody.

Make them proud of you and focus on making their life better, then your life will get better.

> **Find your Fuel! I found mine in Temple Texas. Understand this...**
> **"You are not responsible for your parent's burdens.**
> **Don't judge them ...FIX YOURSELF"**

God has great expectations of you and so do others. You got to change, you got to change today. Toss out the trash in your life, toss out the excuses in your life. Toss out the fear of the unknown in your life

The unknown should be your partner for life.
"The Real" has dealt you knockout blows.
"The Real" has taken your confidence...
"The Real" has discouraged your vision...
Today all that changes... **Today "the unknown" is going to take you to places** "The Real" tried to cheat you out of... Say this, today I will love myself. Today I will love this moment. Today my life has changed for the better. <u>I'm better today because I was in the struggle yesterday.</u>

I've lost some love ones on the way but I'm here to represent those that were lost... I'm here to represent those that love me... Because of them that love me I will not get caught up in silliness or stupidity. I must be focused this year.

I'm washed of anew ...
What does a Hero look like? Hero's look like YOU!
I remember a story of a misunderstood boy.
A boy in the hoodie, that gave his life to save a life. As another boy was drowning in the river, everyone was standing around waiting for someone to save the drowning kid.
While others hesitated, the troubled boy, the hoodie wearing boy, the misunderstood boy dove into the raging water without fear...
<u>"You Get What You Give" in life...</u>

Where did his bravery come from? Maybe from the 28 hours of labor his single parenting mother went thru to deliver him into the world...**The struggle that delivered him** into this world...Was that the key to his bravery...
-Did his mother plant in him the courage?
-Did she plant in him the gift of becoming a hero?
-Did she plant his determination, to hold on to save the drowning boy without letting go?
Her sacrifice at his birth was for his sacrifice that day.

His Mother's sacrifice was the life jacket he needed to swim into the river of everlasting lasting Life, the world of Eternity. Because of his sacrifice to save someone else's life...He became the Man that she planted in him.

<u>*His purpose was served...*</u>

Question-
What's your purpose today?
What's your sacrifice today? What's planted in you? We must look inside of ourselves and see if we can find someone's sacrifice...**We must look inside and see if** we can find someone's courage, someone's bravery...We must look inside to see if we can find someone that we can trust anytime, anywhere, and anyhow. There are no excuses for you...

Your life is not the fault of anyone. Your life is a path of improving you and the path to where you want to go. Just say this today, I have the tools, I have the determination, I have my teachers and my family on my side but if not, so what NO EXCUSES PRODUCES!
I understand –There are dangers out there sending messages of doubt... sending messages of despair... and sending messages of insecurity...But you know what? Someone has already paid for you... You know who he is...

All you need to do is believe...You should believe in HIM and YOU should believe in YOU!

Believe that starting today you're going to be the strongest that you've ever been. You will be the most confident that you've ever been, and you will be the safest that you have ever been in your Life.

TODAY you toss out the trash… you toss out the excuses… and toss out the fear of the unknown. TODAY, the unknown is your partner for life…
    <u>**Believe and whisper this to your heart…**</u>
    I've found my belief …It lives within me…
    You can't see it, but I can feel it…
    You can't feel it but I can touch it…
    You can't steal it…because I own it…
Temple are you ready? Texas are you ready? America you better get Ready!!! Go tell Mama, go tell Granny, tell your Family today I'm finally ready…**Today Change has come**!

I'm a Victory today…This year victory is mine. This is the year of change!!! "Shut up and Get Busy"… **Your time is now…This is your Life follow Your Dreams. Now it's time for you to go…Temple Texas…right here…Go find your dreams…**

                                          Coach Etheridge

> **-TEACHING MOMENTS-**
>
> "A teacher's purpose should be to teach life lessons within their academic study that will enhance the student's life personally. If you don't accomplish both, the student may pass your class, but you are failing the student"

"Build positive relationships, and equip your students, so they will understand that obstacles, conflict, and failures is a part of life. All must be defeated and a great life can be achieved".

"FAILURE IS THE BIGGEST CONTRIBUTOR TO SUCCESS"

If you're not building positive relationships, then you're building obstacles for learning. In many cases TEACHERS are the only pathway to a positive LIFE.

The Day My Life Changed

I finally gained enough confidence to go to the side door of the house and knock. Tap, tap, and tap I tapped softly. My mind began racing with anticipation and fear, all at the same time. In those seconds before the door open my thoughts became questions again. What is he going to look like? Will I look like him? Is he tall, fat, thin, or small? Heck I don't care. I just need to see him! Is he going to be happy to see me? Wait, why has he not talked to me before? I've played in this street all the time. As a matter of fact, this kid on the mini bike could not be his son because his dad left a long time ago. Heck, I don't care; I just need to see my Dad...

"OVERCOME" Words for YOU

The day started normal and hot. But it was a day that would never leave my mind. I was running around playing shirtless in the street, in my worn hand-me-down jeans. Up to that point there had never been a reference to a Daddy in regards to me. My Mom and I had attended school PTA meetings, sporting events, plays, baseball games, football games, free boys club days, bake sales, and every other activity day evented.

Everywhere a young boy goes, he notices that his father is not there. I would always see all the other fathers spending time with their children. I would look at the other children with silent protested envy, so to not alert my mother of my personal turmoil. I always wondered who my father was and longed to have a man to call Daddy.

I ran into the house and ask my Mother for a quarter so I could buy cookies from the store up the street. What she said next changed my life.

"Go on up there to that corner house and ask your Daddy!"

As I walked up the street to the house where the man lived, I began to sweat on top of the normal sweat of the hot summer day. My mind raced in wonderment about what he would look like, and if he would be nice to me. Wait, would he accept me? This is the day that I always had hoped for, however, the moment had somehow come to soon. I felt unprepared for the moment. "I'm not prepared, is this real?"

I was sweaty, a little dirty from playing football in the street and had on raggedy clothes. I was shirtless with dirty worn out tennis shoes. As I approached the gate I noticed a little boy riding a mini bike inside the yard. Wow, my mind began to wonder. My dad must be rich because the boy inside the gate has a mini bike. As I stood there in awe of the boy and the bike, I also noticed someone peeking thru the window of the house. As I watched along the fence line I began to envision me riding the mini-bike and having all kinds of fun. But I noticed as I continued to watch the boy ride, he would ride closer and closer to the fence sort of laughing at me. This did not bother me. I didn't care though because I was about to meet my father.

I finally gained enough confidence to go to the side door of the house and knock. Tap, tap, and tap I tapped softly. Now, I found myself standing at the door of life, manhood, fatherhood...

Tap, tap, and tap I tapped softly. As the door slowly opened, my eyes slowly closed...

I felt the presence of greatness. **This is the best day of my life was racing through my mind.** *I hope I look like him. Then the voice I had waited all my life came thundering through the* blackness of my still closed eyes. A strong base voice ... I trembled in fear and excitement.

"Hey boy, what do you want?"
D d d d d daddy, kc kc kc can I have a q q q q quarter? I stuttered to ask...
**WHAT!?!? Naw!!!
Get your little butt out of here and don't come back!!!**

Did your Mama send you up here? I don't have anything for you... I don't have money... Don't come back up here begging...

For a brief moment I was just happy to hear his voice... The voice of my Dad...Then, **I began to realize the best day of my life was turning into the worst day of my life...**Thoroughly humiliated and deeply wounded. I quickly ran away to the fence crying from the freshly bleeding scare of rejection that marred my heart. After a few minutes my pain became almost unbearable. As I stood at the fence shirtless clenching the metal barbed fence, I then witnessed something even more disturbing. The boy riding the mini-bike suddenly stopped riding. The mini bike was out of gas. The boy threw the bike to the ground, ran to the door of the house and yelled.

"Hey Man! I need some gas for the bike. It's out of gas!"

There was not a twinge of respect in the obviously spoiled boy's voice as <u>he demanded more gas</u>.
<center>I still wanted to trade lives…</center>
The Man/Crusher and that laughing, disrespectful, mini-bike rider… rushed to the car to purchase the gas. The store was located at the corner directly up the street. I watched as they got in the car, drove to the corner store, got the gas, came back and refueled the bike. The Man/Crusher even pulled the rope to start the mini-bike while the spoiled boy began to ride again, laughing at me… I began to think very dangerous thoughts. I was feeling so rejected that I thought about ending it all… After a few minutes my pain became anger and rage. I continued to watch, cry, and hallucinate along the fence line clenching the metal diamond squares with as much grip as a pair of vice grips on a lug nut…

    As I cried and cried, I began to talk to myself. Then all of a sudden the tears stopped. I was screaming inside myself. I then made a couple of promises to God and myself;

    "No matter what happen in my life, I would never allow my future sons or daughters to feel the hatred, I was feeling that day"…I promised myself to never leave my children even if for some reason it doesn't work out with my future wife.

At a young age I decided that I would be a good father and a good husband. The worse day of my life turned into the best day of my life.

"Tragedy can be the Birth of Greatness"

Life is strange some times. Sometimes you just need to survive your darkest moment or night. Most of the time the sunrise the next day is the brightest ever. "You may be bruised but the sun will be Bright"

"I say to you that if that little boy could decide what kind of Man that he was going to become out of that tragic moment, then I know you can do the same." My father and I eventually repaired our relationship. We became really good friends until his death. One of my fondest memories is when he bought me my first car. He wasn't a bad guy at all.

"Sometimes children don't have the capacity to understand adult issues"...

"My Past was Darkness, but my future is Bright. Because my darkest path was somebody's LIGHT"...

"Never hold your head down or let go of the rope. Someone held on because of you, so you must hold on because of them"

TEACHING GREATNESS

"Don't allow any students weakness get in the way of YOUR RESPONSIBILITY to teach them their Greatness"

Don't give up...Don't give in...Don't quit...
Dig in for a ride of resistance...
Dig in for a ride of deflection...
Dig in for a ride to battle insecurity...
Dig in for a ride to fight apathy...

Treat the student's path to success as if it was your child's journey to success...

This is how you become a great teacher. This is how you become a favorite teacher and a valued important teacher...
This is how you become a remembered, inspiring teacher, a Difference Maker.

"Teach to be REMEMBERED...
Don't be REMEMBERED for not teaching"

Coach Etheridge

I'm Not a Statistic

The numbers game will never predict my way.
Insanity on the brain, I don't have time to play.

Statistics and counselors predicting my life
And that I could never change.
I've seen it all and swallowed the pain.

Children that usually survive this circumstance.
Always turn out as victims with a broken stance.

Never again will I be a victim of circumstance,
A product of my environment
Will improve my chance

Determined I am to never strike her face.
My Mothers scare will always fill that space.

What about the turmoil and anger I feel inside.
Will it surface someday?
In what situation will it arise?

The cursing and fighting
Done nothing to heal my heart,
According to statistics and counselors
I'm forever troubled because of that start.

I'm not a statistic and I will never be,
The type of person they expected to see.
Don't look at me with pity or shame.
I'm a boy-to-man in control of his name.

I can't wait to prove you wrong.
I'm not a statistic! It's time to go home.

You juiced my head with excuses to fail.
Not me, my mother's scare taught me well.

Statistics, percentages, and my past
Can't possibly describe the future me
Have the counselors forgotten?
My mom's courage was the key.

God thank you for stepping in,
At a time I really needed a friend.

I'm grown now I made it through.
Quit selling troubled kids fake statistical news.

> **"The one that starts the FIGHT loses himself… But the ONE that FIGHTS for himself finds his Destiny"**

"OVERCOME"

Mr. Z's Words

While reading one of Bruce's stories, it hit me like a ton of bricks. That picture, the one hanging on his office wall. All of the questions about that one particular picture were answered. I looked up and Bruce was staring at me. I asked "is this story about that picture?' Bruce said, "Yes". I had to leave the room because I started to cry. Bruce came out and said to me "It's okay". He was comforting me when I should have been comforting him. I told Bruce, "I can't imagine growing up without a Dad. I love you like a brother". Not only is Bruce a good man, but also a great inspiration to anyone willing to listen to his words.

Mr. Trevino's Words

From the moment I met Bruce or Coach as we all affectionately call him, we had an immediate connection. He is a tremendous listener, has unlimited patience and ability to relate to you and make you feel like you have known him all your life. His message is one of hope, inspiration, caring, sacrifice, acceptance, vision; -it is also a message of self-introspection well worth the journey.

Mr. Noles Words

When it comes to inspirational motivators, Bruce Etheridge is the cream of the crop. Whether in the locker room, the classroom, or the break room, he captivates every audience he's in front of. I've seen Bruce with countless at-risk kids, "coaching them up" to become better sons, daughters, students, brothers, sisters, friends ... better people! On that day (and we've all had them) when nothing seems right, and your get-up-and-go has gotten up and left, pick up this book, flip to any page and read it, soak it in, put yourself between the lines. But consider yourself warned, it might just put you on the path to becoming a better person yourself!

"Many parents take pride in their children looking so much like their father or their mother. The true marking of children is not so much in the similar looks, but more in their excellent behavior".
Mark your children it's never too late...
Gods watching...

The Compress...

I remember one time my Mother told me not to go swimming and I went swimming anyway. The whole time I was swimming, I was in fear of drowning. I knew that I wasn't supposed to be swimming that day so the guilt of disobedience would not let me enjoy the swim. This is a story such as that. I took a short cut to get home walking thru a dangerous area, which my Mom barred me from traveling thru, called <u>"The Compress".</u>

Although "The Compress" would have provided a shorter walking distance to and from my Grandmother's house, my Mom refuse to let us use that route. She understood the dangers...she would say; don't ever go through "The Compress" especially alone because it's too dangerous!

"The Compress" was and area located between the X crossing railroad tracks. It had a dangerous pond in which kids had drowned. It also had a dangerous water tower in which neighborhood kids would climb the ladder to the top, which was very dangerous...It was located in a heavily wooded area with old wirily stretched trees and aluminum building that screeched in the wind. The trees provided shelter and cover for illegal activities and for boys to fight fair fights without interference... The empty trains cars at times would bring in a variety of rough looking men with overgrown beards...The slow moving train would also provide a ride for us to go across town to the boy's club...I knew of a kid that lost his leg catching the train, he slipped off and severed his leg... And finally the rumored Goat Man (half man-half goat) also lived in the area. The Goat Man was rumored to have eaten alive a number of the neighborhood missing children...

There were times that we would use the Compress as a short cut but only when we had a large group of friends for protection from the Goat Man. One day after eight hours of swimming without eating hardly anything but a few crackers and cookies, we had to walk home from the swimming pool. We were hungry, thirsty, tired, ashy, <u>hungry</u>, and <u>thirsty</u>. After walking for about two hours we came to the area of the Compress. The quickest route for me to get home would be to go through the compress.

> Cut thru the Compress...cross thru the uncut field, jump across the Creek... Arrive at home... 25 minutes sooner...

Did I say I was hungry, tired, and thirsty? My friends lived in a different direction so they did not have to go through that area. I was the only

one needing to travel thru the dreaded compress. Well, I could have gone around the long route but I was too tired and hungry.
 I decided to go alone thru "The Compress".

I had the same feeling as I entered the Compress as I did that day I went swimming after my Mom told me not too. "Guilt, Fear, Guilt, Fear, Guilt." As I took my first steps on the compress grounds, I began to hear my Mom's voice saying "Boy, what are you doing! You had better get you little #$% out of the Compress. Don't ever go thru there by yourself.

It had been a bright, hot sunny day, but after I took about ten steps the sun seemed to have disappeared behind the dangerous scary trees scratching the aluminum railroad buildings. The wind began to whisper and the tree limbs began to wave; it was as though I suddenly engaged in a thunderstorm without the rain. The trees presented dangerous shadows, the wind presented whispers of someone (maybe the Goat Man) chasing me. The tree limbs tapping the buildings convinced me that I was definitely in danger.

My mind racing with thoughts of danger, I soon realize **"It's time to run!** I ran so fast my speed sounded like a bullet ricocheting of a building (teeeeeron). I looked back as I ran nearly losing my balance, as I saw a shadowy figure that appeared to be a Man following me. Maybe it was the Goat Man wanting to eat me alive. As I continued to accelerate I soon was faced with a six foot metal gate directly in front of me. No problem, I leaped the gate in a single bound, swinging my legs to the right as my hands lifted my body over the top. After landing on the other side of the gate, I glanced back to see who or what was chasing me. The wind was angry, blowing hard and the dusk dawn darkness refused to tell me.

I then glanced down at my feet. My mind screamed of fear at that moment. There between my feet was a huge black snake coiled up with big red eyes! Did I say between my feet? I stared at the snake; the snake stared back at me. My heart screamed for my Mom internally, but my legs screamed for help. A jolt of adrenaline raced to my heart and legs...like Super Man; I leaped at least fifteen feet on a single bound, landing perfectly like a helicopter. After landing away from the snake I refocused my attention on the dangerous serpent.

The snake (with red eyes) began to uncoil and slither toward my direction. I could not believe my eyes...so I ran away a few steps and stopped to see if he would follow... The snake followed my path; this snake is chasing me! I ran across the railroad tracks and down the hill...I stopped before entering the uncut dumping field. The field had long, tall, uncut weeds and grass. The field also served as an illegal dump spot for trash...There was a narrow walking trail through the middle of the field for safe crossing as long as you stayed on the narrow crossing path. The trail was narrow and long but off the path the grass was higher than I stood. I turned around again to see if the snake was still following me. It was... The snake was slow and patiently chasing after me. I had to run! This snake is after me!

My mind flashed a picture of my Mom heartbroken because I was found dead in the Compress field.

I regained my focus thinking I must get away from this snake! As I began to run down the narrow path...there it was...ANOTHER SNAKE...In the middle of the narrow path way coming towards me. ANOTHER SNAKE was coming from the opposite direction.

I was trapped by two snakes, one in front and one behind me. I was trapped by high grass, mixed with trash and other dumped junk to my left and right. My heart beating faster and faster, I felt as though I was having a heart attack. I was trapped with no place to run. The snakes were closing in on me.

A scene flashed in my mind of a massive search effort by neighbors looking to find me...the missing boy. The front page of the local newspaper reported an unidentified boy's body was found in the Compress field...autopsy showed the boy died from

snake bites and a heart attack... I saw my mother crying in disbelief. She was one hundred percent sure that it wasn't her son that was found, because her son knew better. He knew of the dangers of the Compress.

Moments later I snapped out of the flash scene to discover the two snakes closing in on me. No place to go, my only remaining choice was to run through the junky grass that was taller than my head. I was so afraid of the unknown of the tall grass, but under the circumstances, it was the lesser of two evils. Teeeeeron, thru the grass I streaked. Every step I took I imagined landing on snakes, broken glass, or wood with nails. I jumped every other step to keep my feet from landing on the ground for too long. I felt I was going to die in that field that day. Finally, I made it out of the field. I then jumped across the creek and ran home...

My heart was pounding thru my chest. I could see my shirt thumping. As I burst through the door my Mom sat quietly with a look of concern. She stopped short of asking me what happened. My mom was good at that. Sometimes she would not ask me a question right away so that I would not be tempted to tell a lie. She would wait, and then ask at the right moment. I never told her of that dangerous incident but somehow I think she already knew. My Mom's message became clear that day. Sometimes the shortest way home is the longest way home. Sometimes short cuts can lead to a short life. She wasn't talking about distance or time. She was talking about life...limiting your risk...There are no short cuts to success." Your journey is sometimes more important as your final destiny. The people you meet along your journey will celebrate and attend your wedding, birthdays, graduations, your achievements, and life after death.

My Mom would often say...

Sometimes the shortest way home is the longest way home.

"Sometimes short cuts lead to a short life."

Enjoy the journey and the final destination
"You've got to limit your risk."

Lela Etheridge

"YOUR Failure should be the biggest contributor of YOUR Success"

"Find a Hero in your World first, Then become a Hero in their World"

"Time is valuable, Time really flies, but memories are forever... You should never want to trade your memories for more time" Change a life of regret to a life of RESPECT"

"A brilliant idea or talent trapped inside a lazy mind, is a death sentence for your GREATNESS"

"OVERCOME" Words for YOU

I hope all is well for you. I had a conversation with one of my guys and thought you may need to be reminded this message.

I hope you have your Mom on speed dial... Sometimes mothers make sacrifices that you never know about. Live in the NOW... Not in the PAST...Your best days are yet to come. I truly believe that.

I still believe that you can become the Man your Mom dreamed of. The man SHE envisioned at your birth. Her sacrifice back then, was for your success today. Life is that simple. We choose to complicate life... I remind you again today that

"You are not responsible for your parents BURDENS Don't JUDGE them, FIX yourself"

Troubled Students, Tough Kids can turn out to be leaders of the world. They are fathers, mothers, supervisors, counselors, teachers, coaches, uncles, aunts, cashiers, construction workers, mechanics, bus drivers, car salesmen, educators, analyst, commentators; you name it, just good people...

"WE TOUCH THE WORLD"

Sometimes troubled students or tough kid just needs a chance to survive...revive, and then they start to thrive...

Your role may be to serve as a small simple pathway or a giant pathway to their success. You must be satisfied with your part of their journey. Your part may occur during the most critical moment of the troubled kid's journey. It's easy to become bitter during those critical moments. "Just look at how he's/she's behaving, He or She will never amount to anything"... Stop, that's the moment they need you the most.

"His long lashes attempted to hide,
The hopelessness of life inside his eyes
But a patient one will look and discover inside the eye.
The deep hidden sparkle lurking behind the sty"

Sincerely,
Bruce Etheridge

Thoughts Changes Lives"

"Your worst enemy cannot harm you as much as your own thoughts, unguarded. But once mastered, No one can help you as much"
-THE DHAMMAPADA

YOU MAY NOT HAVE HAD A FATHER GROWING UP, BUT YOUR KIDS CAN HAVE ONE."

"Find a Hero in your World, then become a Hero in their World"

STANDARDS

"SOMETIMES IT'S IMPOSSIBLE TO (GET) RAISE SOMEONE TO MEET YOUR STANDARDS...

SOMETIMES SUCCESS WILL OCCUR IF YOU CAN JUST GET THEM TO LEAVE THEIRS"

TO THE LOVE ONES I LEFT BEHIND...

Your greatness has nothing to do with you being perfect or living perfect. Everyone makes mistakes in their life so don't be too alarmed, that should not be a surprise. We should not wear mistakes as badges of honor but we also should not allow our past mistakes to steal our remaining oxygen either. Quit beating yourself up, your life deserves to have PEACE, HAPPINESS and JOY… Your Greatness lies within you…You must find it, allow it to change you, and allow your greatness to save you.

"OVERCOME" Words for YOU

We all have lost love one's that were dear to our hearts... We've all felt at times that we can't go on... The missing love ones are now watching down on us... We should be grateful to have had the "Missing Love One" for the important moments in our life, the inspiring periods and for their life changing laughter in our lives. Question... Are we lucky or were we BLESSED for their short term Greatness in our lives? Answer...We were blessed to have them. Lost love one's speaks to us every day. The noise of the world will try to drown out, or shut out their voices...don't let it happen...We should listen in our private moments and we should listen in our crying moments. There will be times when we will be awakened by the GREATNESS of those lost. We must recognize those precious voiceless moments of whisper. When you hear...

Hello...I see you wearing the new t-shirts with my pictures on them honoring my life...I see you...but let me say this...If you are wearing them because of REGRET then take them off...If you are wearing t-shirts out of RESPECT then smile and chunk me a "Deuce of Peace"...I SEE YOU... "RESPECT MY LIFE DON'T REGRET MY LIFE"...By the way your happiness is important to me... Hey...you know those hats that I always loved to wear; I smiled when you put one on to take a selfie...by the way your happiness is important to me...Oh yea, I saw you wearing my old house shoes or house coat the other morning...it's cool for you to wear them... just take care of them, they were so comfortable... Thanks for hugging my _____ the other day, I really needed to feel their warmth that day...by the way...I hope you don't mine but I'm living in you... oh yea, by the way I want you to be happy...

I've left so many wonderful memories and wonderful moments to get you through your troubling periods. Focus on those moments and let go of the deadly painful silence. "I'm not in there", I'm not in those dead moments of your search. I'm in your living moments. Please tell my friends to quit looking for me in their PAIN...I'm not hiding in their pain, I'm riding a new PAINLESS GOLDEN LANE... Ask them not to seek me in pain or anger, but tell them to seek HIM for forgiveness. Tell them the time is now for them to "Get right, Get ready, and get busy...

My life is among your living, I'm in your midst. The time is now for all to look forward, move forward, and seek the power of God's greatness. You have the children in your midst, you have our family in your midst, and you have my most valued possessions among you. Your happiness is still at the top of my list... You feel your life is a mess... **"STOP THAT!"** You, our family, and the children are my BEST... I need for you to take care of yourself in my physical absence. I cry for your happiness because I'm happy...I'm okay, I'm in great hands (SMILE)...

Please tell my friends that are hurting; tell them not to dwell in PAIN... It's time for them to seek a better life. Also tell them to keep wearing the hats and t-shirts to remember lost love ones but also seek to wear the uniforms of their own responsibility. I've made some mistakes but I've been forgiven. The most important claim I ever made was to claim Jesus. As I see the struggles of the world, I must tell you that someone has already paid for your HAPPINESS. He paid the ultimate price for you...Don't give your happiness away because of guilt.... Start today...#1...by taking care of you, only then will you be able to take care of others..."You can't attain your GREATNESS, until you attend to your GREATNESS"

PS...Hug my family today...Be happy today, and talk to Jesus today...He is the key to our Greatness...

Shut Up and Get Busy!!!
"There inside the Hoodie was Greatness!"

If you think your life is tough. Check this out. I know a kid that had a tough life. During his middle school and high school years his mother and father was in prison (same time on occasions). His brothers and nephew was in and out of jail also. His oldest brother got out of prison, got shot five times, lost an eye, then returned to prison. Yet, this kid never gave up. He went on to graduate from high school with his class, then, graduated from college. He became a teacher and coach to make a difference for others.

Keys to his success:

He found an interest...Basketball and Positive Activities

He found a mentor...His Coach

He believed in a "I'm No Victim Attitude"

He got Busy with his Future!!!

He is an American Hero

I'm close to the
edge,
I may fall off...
No one to catch me,
I hope the end is
soft...
Get away from the
edge
Mom would say
time and time again

I need you safe and
sound
It's time to find
new friends...

"OVERCOME" Words for YOU

Fa_r_ther Needed

A Boy without a Father
Will search quick and fast
To find the Man that did not last...

He will run, hustle, and find the game
To replace the lost fathers crime,
He'll never be the same.

The Boy will accept fast money
and a dead end plan
Because he didn't have his #1 fan
To help him refuse temptation,
and to withstand

Today I will evaluate my own plan
Thanks Mom, I understand

Your voice now clear, I hear your advice,
Better choices are on the way because
I finally understand your sacrifice...

"Message"

If you had 5 million dollars would you burn it? People work hard every day to get money, make money, and hustle money. Your talent can make more money than your hustle ever will. You are talented in drawing. I would rather say you are a talented artist not a talented drawer.

"Don't waste a $5 million dollar talent on a $20 hustle"

Race Time Choice
(Excerpt)

Running the race based on race, is a race that's difficult to run. But a race, racing forward is a race already won.

Timing of time is important all the time.
If the times aren't timed, hard times will be multiplied times, when the good times are mine.
Choose chosen if choice was your choice to be,
Chosen is the choice that chooses yourself you see

If success and failure are both choices, choose to focus on Success…It makes you feel better…

"OVERCOME" Words for YOU

Complete the Man!!!

He wasn't there, it's just not fair.
He wasn't there, it's just not fair.

I searched doors all over looking for the key.
I needed an answer to the question of
Why my Dad wasn't there for me.

My mind confused by denial and rejection,
only made me more determined to
Seek his affection.

Take time to find yourself my Mom would often say.
Because I felt incomplete
I continued to search for that Runaway.

The Runaway was not a Runaway you see.
He was a decent Fade-away
That didn't agree with me.

An unclaimed son I feared was the answer,
my blood boiling and poisoned like a deadly cancer.

I searched the darkness only to find
Heartache and pain
Looking to find the missing tool to make me sane

I was like a chipped plate or a cracked glass.
A broken tool that would not last

I was like a broken wrench that could not grip,
the harder I turned the more I slipped…

I raced through life, a race without a finish line.
Son slow down, Son, these things take time.

My greatest blessing delivered my son you see.
Damn, wow my boy looked just like me.

My seed sprouted my Son was bare.
But because of my confused journey,
His future tainted with despair.

The seed grew older confused and never finishing.
Looking over his shoulder
For something that seemed to be missing

You deserved better from me,
Because you were there
Together, forever thru the memories we shared.

Live life abundantly my final request
Find PEACE, LOVE and don't be afraid to invest.

The past cannot be changed,
Many mistakes I made.
My burdens are not yours Son;
Your path has been paid.

I'm watching from all high, Son
In my Fathers hand
Son now is the time for you to
Complete the Man...

In Memory of Joel Darnell Kindred

"CATCH THAT FLY"

There will be times in your life when someone you love will not believe in the vision that you will have. This does not mean that they do not support you; it could simply means that you're growing towards your purpose. There will be times when your closest friends or relatives will be the obstacle stunting your growth. Sometimes the only vision to success you need is yours; others may not be able to see nor understand your vision or purpose. God has a vision and a purpose for you.

The frustrations of a difficult losing basketball season had taken its toll. Sometimes fans, and parents, and friends, can be rude and disrespectful. It's part of the coach's responsibility to handle that. As you can imagine the toll of such criticism on anyone eventually can distract any coach from his principles, his vision, and his purpose. As I was working in my office I was feeling a little down. I was feeling a little (mighty low) underappreciated as my young son, (I believe eight your old) came into my office play in his usual manner. Winning games or losing games didn't matter to him because he had unlimited access to his hero. His normal routine was to be around his father. I loved it because he reminded me of my purpose with my players, my purpose with my position, and my purpose to serve. Under what seems to be turbulent circumstances, coaches should always understand and never to lose sight of their true purpose.

1) We must train young boys or girls to become great men or women
2) We must work hard, laugh harder, and respect each other and others…
3) We must become great fathers, regardless of any situation or circumstance…
4) We must win as many games as we can without breaking interfering with any of the first three rules…

"To coach or teach is the greatest position I was told.
"To coach, to teach, to motivate
A balanced young man or woman must unfold."

"Daddy can I play in your office" he said. Sure son, but I'm going into the storage room to put away the uniforms and other equipment for a few minutes. I'll be back in about 10 minutes. "Okay Dad" he replied. I left my office door open so that I could hear him in case if he needed me. My office was simple, four walls, and a desk (with stapler and tape dispenser) with computer, and book shelves full of trophies, file cabinet, common items in every coach's office.

The door led directly into the hallway. Anyone walking down the hallway could peer into the office as they strolled by without interference. Most students would use my open door as an excuse to speak (Hello Coach) and get free candy from my desk. Remember it had been a struggling season; two years had passed since our last championship. Parents, administration, and a few friends were even second guessing. It's amazing how good of a coach you are when you have good players, and how bad a coach you are when you have good kids but not as talented. So you can imagine I had a lot of pent up frustration and anger from the lack of respect for my past success.

So after working in the storage room I returned to the office to check on my son. As I walked into my office my son was standing with one leg on top of my desk other on top of the file cabinet. He was holding with two hands a strip of clear tape. In the ten minutes I was away, he had begun his quest. Shoe prints were everywhere…papers scattered on the floor…wall pictures slanted and unbalanced… championship trophies tipped over or leaning inside the shelves.

Son, what are you doing?

I scream in my strongest voice to the top of my lungs. Get down, if you get hurt your Mother will blame me!…I was so upset…as he jumped down and returned to the floor I noticed the strip of tape still lodged in his two hands, between both index fingers and thumb. Then as I tried to regain my composure I began to look around the office and noticed that my son, my first born, had what seemed to be more than 100 strips of tape on each wall, on the desk, on the cabinets. My son had placed strips of tape everywhere in my office. I'm sure more than 400 hundred tiny strips of tape had been placed on the walls. As he began to explain, I interrupted…At that moment of course my anger had gotten the best of me, I lost it. I began to scold him in a way he had never witness. **What's wrong you Son are you stupid? Why, why, shut up! You must be @##$%^& or something…** Oh my, the office door has been open…did anyone see you doing this crap…How can you be so dumb…people are going to think you stupid. In his eyes, a rain storm of tears; in my eyes, a raging hurricane of anger. As I continued to belittle him, humiliate him, and confessed it to anyone within voice range of his ridiculous game of taping the wall. Then as any good father would do I paused for a moment to listen to his reasoning. What he said next sent me even further into the frustrating rage of the losing season.

<u>**"I was trying to catch a fly"**</u>.

WHAT!!!Oh my goodness, Lord what's wrong with this boy?

SON, YOU CAN'T CATCH A FLY WITH TAPE!!!

Son, get this mess cleaned up NOW…I'm going back into the storage room and I will be back in ten minutes and you had better have this office in perfect condition…

Get every piece of tape off this wall… DO YOU HEAR ME?

I then left my office to returned to the storage room to work (really it was to find a private moment to pray for him…lol) well after about 10 minutes I heard a loud thunderous sound of someone falling in my office area. "Oh Lord this boy has killed himself" raced through my mind. As I raced out of the storage room toward my office I screamed his name…He raced out of my office toward the storage room he screaming my name…We passed each other out of panic…I stopped and grabbed him looking for the bloody nose or a broken arm or some type of life threatening injury (I really mean wife threatening injury). I grabbed him and as I began to check him… He screamed at me…I did it Dad, I did it. What, what did you do? What did you break? Are you okay? No Dad, I'm okay, I did it… Shut up boy!

"I DID IT!!! I CAUGHT THAT FLY DAD"

At that moment he reached into his pocket and remove a strip of tape…there in the middle was...

"A BLOODY FLY".

I paused to try to understand…I began to cry…I began to tremble… I began to regret. He was so excited that I'm not sure he recognized my disappointment. As I began to apologize to him over and over, I began to wonder why I treated my own son in such a manner. I did to him what others were doing to me as a coach. Was it the frustration of a losing season? Yes it was. At times our frustrating circumstances control our decisions. We unleash anger on those we love. Sometime words can hurt more than physical punishment.

In that instant, I looked into his eyes twenty years down the road. Never again will this happen I promised him and myself. I relived all the negative comments, the harsh words, the words of anger, the words of embarrassment, and the ugly words from his hero over and over in my mind. What surely would have broken me at a young age didn't break him because he believed. He locked his faith. Although his spirit was temporarily broken, it was only temporary. I was wrong. You must believe in yourself even when others don't. YOU must ignore the critics of those closest to you and proceed on with God's plan. Can you do that today? You must refuse to quit even as others laugh or fail to understand your vision. Can you do that today, tomorrow, or that right NOW… It time for you to go and catch your fly…Just don't step on the important papers please… God bless you…

SON, YOU CAN CATCH A FLY WITH TAPE!!!I was wrong!!!

Uniforms

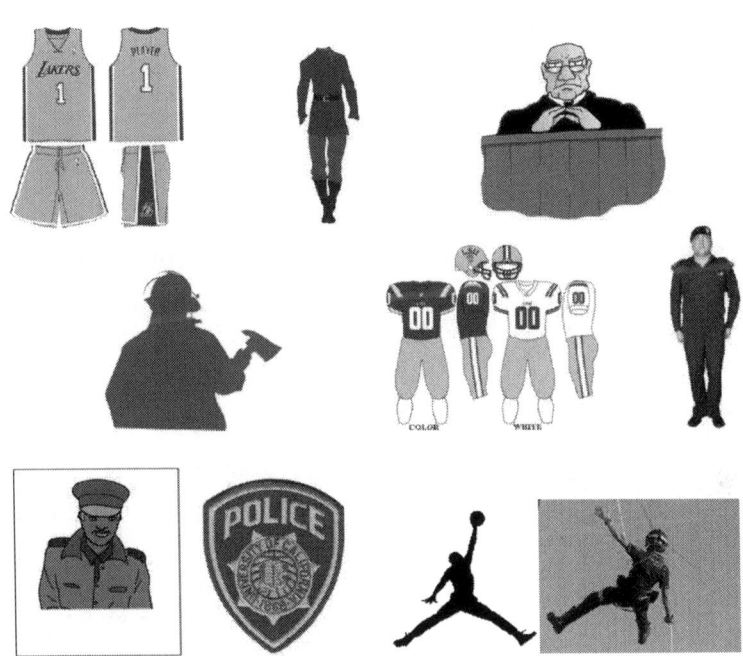

Uniforms don't make HERO'S...
Service in UNIFORMS DOES...
Service to OTHERS makes a Hero!
SERVICE...SERVICE!!!

"OVERCOME" Words for YOU

"The Shaded Legacy Tree"

Another one gone, why does it have to be?
A life claimed by the streets to be buried under "The Shaded Legacy Tree"

A lynching ROPE of hopelessness, anger and despair
Continues to lynch, hang or choke, the new ROPE don't care

The streets, drugs, and the hustle, teammates for LIFE
Even family, friends, or hugs couldn't stop the STRIFE

Racing through of life, trading young life for old shaded DIRT
Why? Why? Why? Why shame your family? Why shame your BIRTH?

Lost opportunities, anger, the streets, the new shackling CHAINS!
Darkness is here…no one controls the STREETS stupid GAMES

Fake cigars and miracle drugs allowing your mind to DOZE
But miracle words, the miracle of you… never to be EXPOSED

Puppet people, claimless claims, and false KIN
Replacing PASTORS, birth names and true family and FRIENDS

Minimization and confusion, where good is bad and bad is GOOD
Now maximum confusion for minimal minds, hatred like the coned HOOD

Selling, claiming, sagging, and bagging as the world takes a STAND

Wake up son! Get your chin and your pants up God also gave you a DEVINE PLAN

The streets are tough… the street will ravage your SIGHT
We tried to tell you God's word would win all your FIGHTS?

C-Note, Fat Killa, or Sexy P, all names purchased in the STREETS
Names that led to rough beds, now your face covered by the SHEET…

All lost…your name, your purpose, and your mother's sacrificed BIRTH
Puppets shouting street names as your bed of dirt began shifting the EARTH

Flip a coin, flip a coin right now! I hope it lands on HEADS
I hope you're ready today…God called heads…he's making someone's BED

Your greatness gone but in FAMILY you will always PREVAIL
Thanks for the gift but we would rather have you…Damn, sorry we failed

My, My, My… I still remember…my Grandmother would often SAY
I didn't understand the WHY back then…but I understand the my, my, my TODAY

Another one gone…Why does it have to be?
Today we sit, talk, and drink tea under "The Shaded Legacy Tree"

"OVERCOME" Words for YOU

"Man, I'm not changing for anyone!"

What if?

"Okay, if you don't change,
You're going to get yourself killed.
Or
"Okay, if you don't change,
Your Mom needs to plan your funeral!
Or
"Okay, if you don't change.
You're going to lose your wife!

Oh.....Change made....

"I change a little every day for the ones I Love..."

Shut Up and Get Busy!!!

If you think your life is tough. Check this out, I know a WOMAN that survived a tough, tough period in her life. During some dark days this person lost her father; a year later she lost her mother, a few months later she lost her brother, and then a few months after that, she lost her sister. Yet, this person never gave up. She survived and continued to thrive in education to make a difference for others.

Keys to her success:

She found an interest... Returned to College...

She allowed friends to support and help her during the tough times...Didn't Shut others out...

She believed in a "I'm No Victim Attitude"

She got BUSY with her Future!!!

She is an American Hero

Women are a lot TOUGHER than Men....
Men are just ROUGHER...

"OVERCOME" Words for YOU

> "Physical and Emotional stability both go hand in hand. Physical Greatness with an emotional scar, develops a Dangerous Man"

> "Coaches are entrusted with family jewels in tacked. The jewels should be returned without a permanent crack"
>
> **Excerpt from "Coaches' Clause or Claws"**

"To the young coaches, getting a new start Be yourself, do what's right. Follow your own, NOT someone else's hardened heart."

YOUR GREATNESS WILL BE REMEMBERED

Something you need to know about kids
I'm reminded every day of the gifted memories that children will have of you. Even in their darkest hour, or happiest moment, they will remember person that tried. They will say, as KIDS often say, that you were mean at times, they will say that you were mad a lot, they will say that they felt your disappointment,

BUT as ADULTS they will say

"Thank you God for my _____".
They will say: I remember when...
They will say: Do you remember the time we....
They will say: Because you were there so I must do this for her/him...
They will say: I must name my 1st born after this Great person...

The trouble child never forgets the one that got them thru or the one that tried. Your most glorious years are soon to be...Your reward was not to win every battle, but to win the WAR...

I HOPE THAT IS ENOUGH FOR YOU...

We all must learn to let go of the distilled water of the past that has lost its taste and has no flavor. And drink of the fresh sparkling water God sends to quench our thirst, which is full of flavor and satisfaction...

"I Cry Everyday"

"OVERCOME" Words for YOU

Always Hug'em First
Always Make'em Smile First
Then proceed....

"The Best thing I ever read was... "The students sitting in the Desk"

Ya Who, Who Ya Who Who!!!
Oh yea...and you better respect your Mama...

Never be ashamed of who you are or where you come from..."Unfortunate Beds, make Brilliant Heads"

"Nurture their wounds past their shackles"...

MESSAGE FOR STRUGGLING YOUNG STUDENTS ATTENDING SCHOOL...

You are not there to discover drugs, thugs, nor inappropriate hugs...You are not there to fight, claim gangs, tag, judge, nor participate in immature conversations...Quit tripping... hoping to be accepted by others...

YOU WERE ACCEPTED ON THE DAY OF YOUR BIRTH...

Drugs may dull the pain today, but will surely bring the pain and anguish tomorrow. You need to quit acting up...quit acting out...quit trying to be hard... There are a lot of hard people in grave yards buried under soft dirt...leaving their love ones lost, hurt, and crushed as they ask themselves why... Remember... You are there to discover your path for success... You are there to discover hope for your future and to frame a better you.

"If you have GREATNESS at HOME...Bring it to school with you for others to DISCOVER in you...

If you have trash at HOME, Leave it at HOME... Come to school to DISCOVER YOUR GREATNESS"

"OVERCOME" Words for YOU

I'm a HEro

I'm a HEro, I promise to take care of my children...

A HEro is not perfect, he has flaws, he may even stumble
He will get up, fix himself, learn from mistakes to become humbled

Heroes rise up, refuse temptation, and never quit for silly reasons.
Refusing a quitters taste during a raging bitter season.

NOTHING precedes responsibility; the children must come first...
I must plan for their future; I must quench their thirst...

I understand my past now, but the future belongs to them...
Parents must give of themselves to build the self of the children...

There will be no excuse, forever to be a HEro ...
The path lost fathers create, dysfunctional children of a lost Zero...

I understand my DAD value because of my own experiences you see...
Where I am today is because I remember where I use to be...

Regretful decisions, silly mistakes, the children not one of them
Happy to be a HEro, their father, God rewarded me with her and him!

Zeroes are afraid, they run away and they escape the scene,
Leaving behind filthy scares and dirty wrinkles that need to be cleaned
Children must be cleaned; their troubled path must be relieved.
I promise never to leave, I promise never to deceive

No longer lost in anger or despair nothing to get in our way.
My children needs a HEro, I must find a way to stay...

I may have stumbled out of the gate in others eyes...
But never a Zero to my children...only a HEro in their clear blue skies

Yesterday, we held hands, hers were soft, his gently and kind.
But tomorrow's life, a better life...to be understood in due time...

Don't judge me; just be happy to know...
Today you hear the voice of a Man...You hear the promise of a HERO

Write It Down

I hope to become a _____. For me to become a _____.

    A) I must improve myself in the following categories. My success lies in these critical important areas.

1 Attitude   2 Behavior   3 Language

    I must rid myself of negative thinking; however other issues that I struggle with are;

  1
  2
  3

C) I must fix my relationship with the following people;

  1
  2
  3

Here is my story/plan of change-

D) The Education required becoming a_____

-Check One-

Dropout__   HS Grad__   Certification__   Tech College__   2yr College__   4yr College__   MS Degree__

Summarize A, B, C, and D (on back of page)

I realize that I cannot do this alone, so I plan to ask _____ to be my mentor.
I understand that I will not be perfect, and may make a mistake along the way, but I plan to give my best effort.
I must make _____ proud of me.

_____Signatures -Date-

What Does A Hero Look Like?

I remember an incident when I was young boy that never left me. There was a troubled neighborhood kid that everyone seemed to believe or assumed that he was a bad kid. **He wore a hoodie most of the time to cover his troubled life.** Even good people have a tendency to hate on something they can't explain.

Sometimes troubled kids are confused with bad kids. There is a huge difference between troubled kids vs. Bad kids.

The Hoodie wearing troubled kid kept to himself and seemed angry all the time, so most viewed him as a bad person. He was a tall, slim, athletic looking boy but had a very edgy attitude and demeanor. He didn't smile a lot or appear to ever be happy. Even his peers were sort of nervous around this troubled kid. He did not have a problem with fighting, or confrontation and to most that knew him; he left an imprint of uncertain danger or bad news. "Don't hate on something you can't explain. Any youngsters wearing Hoodies at 2am will breed fear and uncertainty to others. Right or wrong, that's the fact. People are often intimidated of the unknown. Jeff was a kid such as this. Not much was known about "Jeff the Troubled Kid", but soon all that would change.

One summer a group of boys took a trip to the river to play and swim. I believe the trip was a reward for a successful baseball season... All the boys were playing, swinging, swimming and having so much fun. It was a beautiful day; the sun was smiling at the clouds, the birds were chirping at the trees, and the boys was laughing and smiling at daylight.

A little distance up the river, danger was lurking. The river itself was a creation of the lakes Dam, a few miles up the river. On the outside of the lake was a huge cemented Dam that appeared to be a cemented grave for the flood gates. I always noticed the Dam because it was the perfect riding surface for crazy insane skateboarders. The Flood gates would open from time to time to lower the water level of the lake. Most of the time the flood gates were closed which provided great fishing spots for the local fishermen. Before Flood Gates would open a siren would sound for an extended period of time to warn those using the river for fishing or swimming.

The boys were swimming a couple of miles down the river away from the flood gates. The Sirens began screaming at the clear blue sky. The boys were having so much fun that their ears did not hear the warning sirens screaming thru the sky. At first, the rising currents made the swim and the swimmers more excited. Then, Mr. Panic stepped in and warned them to get out of the

"OVERCOME" Words for YOU

water. As the boys struggled to swim to shore, the turbulent rambling, currents swept most of the boys further down the river. The water was too strong and dangerous for the boys to withstand.

Most of the boys got out of the river safe except for Kerry. Kerry was the one boy that could not escape the muscle of the rushing water. Everyone else was out of the water except for Kerry. Kerry surfaced enough for us to see him briefly.

"Jeff the troubled Kid" jumped into the water without hesitation to save Kerry.

As Jeff swam toward Kerry, Kerry went under for the second time...Jeff chased Kerry through the swift current, under the water to grab him...Jeff was able to grabbed Kerry only by the hair on his head and scrambled up to the rumbling surface. Kerry panicked from the strong grip to his head and the rushing water in his throat and began to fight for his life.

Kerry fought for his life...
Kerry pushed up, he pushed down, and he pushed away. Kerry panicked and began to scratch and claw the arm of Jeff. Kerry's finger nails dug deep into his rescuer's arm.

Still, Jeff refused to let go of Kerry.
Moments later both boys went under the raging current for a third time...Then a few seconds later both Jeff and Kerry appeared again for a brief and final moment, as if to say goodbye, and then both were swept away to better swimming hole that I call the....

..."River of Everlasting Life"

I will never forget Jeff and the sacrifice he made for Kerry. I hope to see him again and to be a better friend. I had nightmares for years dreaming about that tragic moment when Jeff and Kerry went away. Jeff was the type of kid that not many people would have a lot of good to say. But, how many of those judgmental people (haters) would have made the ultimate sacrifice that Jeff made for Kerry?

"Don't Hate On Something You Don't Understand."

After his death everyone began to understand Jeff's unfortunate life. He was misunderstood, frustrated, troubled, and faced unfair criticism from elders and his teachers. He had unbelievable odds against him. That inner turmoil pitted against his unrecognized courage, his misunderstood bravery and compassion: was a bigger tragedy than the accident in the river.

Jeff was sent to us to teach us the ultimate lesson; Write the lesson you feel Jeff taught you in one of the space pages. So when I ask you "What Does a Hero Look Like"? The faces of many people come to my mind, my grandmother, my mother, King, Kennedy, Ali, and Jeff and Kerry comes to my mind also. Kerry taught us how to fight for life and to give it your best shot. Jeff taught us be unafraid of making the ultimate sacrifice for others. **"You get what you give."**

Jeff gave his life then gained Eternal Life.

"OVERCOME" Words for YOU

Man in the Mirror

As I look in the mirror this morning to prepare my face, to comb my hair, to brush my teeth, and to make sure that I look good today, I pause for a moment to pray and talk to you today Lord. Today as I look into the mirror, I promise I will search for your goodness in me and your kindness in others...

Today Lord as I work outside, I will cut edge and trim. I will cut the grass, trim the bushes, and edge the sidewalk. I will also cut the excuses out of my life and trim my attitude. I will speak quietly, and listen intently... After carefully edging the sidewalk, I will do the same with you, walking by your side on the straight and narrow. I promise to straighten out my life.

Today, my greatest dreams will become reality. I will become the Man my mother envisioned at my birth. The boy she sacrificed for has finally begun to repay his eternal debt. My mother's dreams and expectations will become reality.

After today, I will no longer be the lost longing dream of my mother or grandmother. I will no longer be the little boy of yesterday's disappointments and nightmares. Today I've finally decided to become the Man they dreamed of. I'm leaving the troubled boy that I made, to become the man they envisioned, the man my mother planted...

Today Father God as I go to the grocery store to purchase food or drive thru the drive thru, so that I can be full...I will also try to fill others with the abundance of forgiveness, compassion and respect because of you. I will plant the seeds of forgiveness, compassion, and respect in all the fields for future growth.

Today, as I drive I will be careful to travel at a safe speed. I will purposely use the signals lights to alert others of my direction. In the darkest hours I will also warn others of the dark turns and slippery curves that are ahead, I will warn their darkness with light of Jesus.

Today I will warn of the dangers of not obeying YOU. Not obeying your traffic lights; not watching out for your low water crossings and your dead end roads. I will also warn of the grave danger of running YOUR stop signs. I hope that others will stop. I hope that others will stop the nonsense, stop the silliness, and stop the stupidity. My hope is many will slam on the brakes to stop the negative language of despair, and the detrimental thoughts of the lost.

As I stop at the rail road crossings and the flashing red lights today Father, I realize in Jesus name that I must be patient. I must be patient with others and I must be patient with you.

Today, I also must confess that I get tired sometimes. Sometimes I need a troubling day nap...I know there are many others out there growing tired also. They feel have no place to rest or no time to rest...

"OVERCOME" Words for YOU

They are too afraid to slow down and too afraid to look back. Some Are So Tired, That They Want To Give Up And Sleep Forever. But you will not allow that. The sacrifice of cross will not allow us to quit... Father God, carry us thru our raging storms.

Father you are telling me that it's not my time. There is someone more important needing me to survive this moment of darkness. Someone else needs me more than I need myself. I can't be selfish today. I will not rob Peter to pay Paul. I will not cheat my love ones or my family to reward the Devil...

My life may be a raging storm right now full of hail of uncertainty, full of hurricane wind of anguish but I know you are with me...you are my life raft to safety. I know that you have left room for my survival. Your plan is for me to survive this moment because young eyes are watching. Father, I know you are supplying all the strength and protection needed for my survival. I know that you want me to survive today. I know you want my family to survive also so we can thrive tomorrow.

Well Lord, it's time for me to go now and face the world... My mirror seems different now since we've spoken today... As I look into the mirror I no longer see my wants but I see your needs... I'm ready for the world... I must go now because someone is waiting on me to save them...

My Mother's Family
"Being raised in a single parent household has given me unlimited fuel for success"

"My Mother and Grandmother gave me an Alternative Fuel"

"GREATNESS HAS NOTHING TO DO WITH LIVING A PERFECT LIFE; BUT A LIFE OF IMPACT HAS EVERYTHING TO DO WITH GREATNESS"

Grandson

Grandmother- A Moment of Silence

Show respect by silently standing and reflecting during a Moment of Silence.
Our mind's often reflecting of hero's, some lost to violence.

Ali, Kennedy, and Dr. King "Greats of All Time",
Add my Grandmother to the list.
She was great and truly "One of a kind."

Her message of Love was relentless, thunderous, and sometimes foggy.
Those that weathered the storm really won the Lottery.

Unselfish LOVE, the binding message from this Great Mother
Love, Honor, Help, but don't judge your Sister or you Brother…

Forgive, Forgive, Forgive, Be brave, strong, and be kind to kin.
Her powerful message, we should begin and end.

She touched so many, her examples never better.
Today remember her legacy, from this tribute letter.

Respect the Silence in the Moment,
The moment is not mine
The moment is for my grandmother,
Please show respect, and remember it's her time.

You've really grown into your presence...We can't wait to see growth in your purpose.

Each day spend more time appreciating the now, the today...Spend a little less time dreaming of tomorrow and focus on doing today.

Active day's make attractive tomorrows...
Inactive day's make reactive tomorrows
Be Active,
Be alert,
And be eager each day!!!

His Smile

When I was a little boy, this man smiled at me... I needed it, I smiled back....

When I (the boy) became a teenager, this man smiled at me... I needed it, I smiled back....

When I (the teenager) became a man, this man smiled at me again... I needed it, I smiled back.

Even now, I still remember his needed smile...

I awoke this morning happy and smiling because of this Man...

As I looked into the mirror, I noticed his gift; I know he wanted you to have it.

Now I realize why he smiled at me all those years, it was so I could give it to you today, you need it. (His smile)

"His smile made a difference in my life"... I thank God for That Man's needed smile...

Today I send you his smile... "You Need It"...

Fa<u>r</u>ther Needed

A Girl without a Father will search farther and farther to find her Father...

She will search, find, an accept an empty Man without a plan

Because her Father wasn't there to teach her to take a stand...

Today I stand, determined to take a stand and to make good choices

Girls must be prepared...This is the quote used to motivate fatherless daughters... great girls... Girls and Boys must be reminded to define their own greatness. Don't adopt the weakness or excuse of the missing parent...

YOUR GREAT...HE'S LATE!

"OVERCOME" Words for YOU

I was totaling my bills the other day...I figured out that I still owe my Mother Slightly more than

1 Billon Dollars

...

Thank God she accepts payments

....

" I'm so lucky to make payments every month without hesitation"

"I hate my mother"
Because she abandoned me
She left me without caring...

Stop right there!

She may have left you to save you...
Maybe she wasn't in the right mindset to raise you safely

Maybe you are here TODAY,
Because she left you To SAVE YOU!

The tragedy of abandonment was the "Birth of Your Greatness"

Quit Making Excuses

"Why do you want people to hear your EXCUSE?
You should want people to see your USE"
I SPEAK THIS TO THEIR WORLD!

SOMETIMES TOUGH WORDS IS NEEDED TO AWAKEN THE SOUL...

Shut Up and Get Busy!!!

If you think your life is tough. Check this out. I know a kid that had a tough period in his life. He went off to college and made more than a couple of mistakes. He was suspended from college, returned to his hometown as a disgraced under achiever. I phone him to check on him. He was so happy to hear from me.

"Coach, I was going to call you with my good news. I'm back in college to get my coaching degree. I'm really focused now on raising my new born son. I know I've made some mistakes but that's not going to stop me from being a good Father to my son. I've changed and I know being a good father is more important than my past mistakes."

He's becoming a teacher and coach to make a difference for others.

Keys to his success:

He admitted, "I've made some stupid mistakes, but I'm not stupid...

He forgave himself of his past...

He remembered that Fatherhood takes precedent over all else...

He got BUSY with his Future...

He is an American Hero

STYLES

"IF YOU CAN MAKE THEM SMILE, THEY WILL GO THE EXTRA MILE IF YOUR STYLE CREATES A FROWN, DIFFICULT TEACHING AND LITTLE LEARNING WILL GO DOWN"

"Being a Father Is Rough at Times.
But Being a Motherless Child is like being in the path of a Category 5 HURRICANE
Every escape route leads to Tragedy"...

Mama ooooh Mama

"OVERCOME" Words for YOU

It's Your Passion Not Your Position

Sometimes Students need MORE than They Deserve!

More

Love **Compassion** **Patience**

Chances **Attention** **Understanding**

"Making MISTAKES is a part of LIFE."

"Be a blessing to someone as you go on your way.
But remember to whisper to

HIM

While working today"

Being different isn't
always bad.
But, if bad is different
a child will be sad.

Being different may
just be good.
Especially to those
who were born
and raised in the
Hood

The Bully

When I was young most of the elementary kids walked to school every morning. We would laugh, race, throw rocks at birds, and talk along the way. The lucky kids needed to arrive a little earlier because they were chosen to be crossing guards. Wow, they would get to wear the cool bright orange vest and hold the Stop sign, the ultimate reward for good behavior.

Located a mile away from the elementary school was a Junior High school (now called Middle Schools). The elementary and middle school kids often walked the same path to school. This was not the best situation for younger students because the older middle school students often would fight, curse, or display some type of inappropriate behavior of some sort. Most of the students was on free lunch program but needed extra money for extra milk or roll. My mother would give me thirty-five cents for lunch every day to cover the cost for extra milk and roll. We played so hard during recess, extra milk and roll was needed for fuel.

The trouble started when this "Big Eight Grader" started taking the younger kids lunch money on his way to middle school. "Joe the Bully" would jump out of the alley and scream "Give me your lunch money"!

Most of the terrified elementary kids would reach into their pockets to accommodate the Bully. Sometimes we would run away or attempt to run away, but he would hit the caught students, because the others ran. So at times depending on who was caught we would not run to save his prisoner from further punishment. He was so big and scary looking, the elementary students were happy to trade lunch money vs. a smack in their little face. We even tried to walk different routes to avoid "Joe the Bully". His GPS always seemed to know our path, so the collector still showed up to take our lunch money no matter the route. This went on for months and months. I would be starving when I got home from school and my mother would ask "Boy, did you eat at school today? Why are you so hungry?"

My cousin, who was same age as me, moved back to the United States from Japan. His Dad was in the military and was being station back home. I was so happy to see him because we had so much in common. We were like "two peas in a pod. He enrolled at the same elementary school until their family could get their housing situation settled. Wow, we (Mark and Bruce) were so happy to be attending the same school together. My Mom and Aunt would not let us have the same class because we would have never learned anything in the same class.

"OVERCOME" Words for YOU

On our first walk to school, I was so excited to be with my cousin, I somehow forgot to warn Mark of the daily robbery routine. So as the group (including Mark and myself) walk to school, "Joe the Bully" jumped out of the alley. All the young elementary kids ran, which was our normal routine. I looked back to see who he had caught before deciding if I needed to keep running or not. There, walking slowly and confidently was my cousin Mark. Mark yelled to me "Bruce, why are you running?" I screamed, Mark come on! He's going to take your lunch money. Mark replied, No way! He's not getting my milk money. This is mine; my Mama gave me this money. Mark continued to walk right by "Joe the Bully". "Joe the Bully" gristly looked at Cousin Mark and realized he was an unafraid new kid. Joe then ignored him and went on to the next kid, victimizing the next kid of his pocket change.

After we got to school, I was embarrassed that I had been afraid. My cousin Mark explained "Don't ever give him your lunch money again, if the rest of our family ever found out they would kick your butt" (meaning my own family would beat me up for being a coward). Okay, I said, I won't run again. Mark then said, I'm going to tell Lawrence (Lawrence was my older cousin that was an 8th grader at the same middle school as "Joe the Bully). I'll bet he won't bully us again. When Mark said that, my stomach tightens to a knot and I became nervous. Mark and I walked to school the next day together, away from the other students. My cousin Lawrence followed us, walking about a half a block behind us, trailing waiting to see if "Joe the Bully would intercept the pockets of his coin factory. As we passed the ally, I struggled to walk and breathe. I was nervous of the conflict that was to come. I was hoping that "Joe the Bully" was sick or something, because I did not want to face him. My cousin Mark walked with the confidence of a young Denzel Washington.

Then it happened, "Joe the Bully" jumped out of his same usual hiding spot but for some reason, I was still surprised. "Give me your lunch money, he demanded". A half second later "Joe the Bully" was on the ground being pummeled with left hooks and right jabs, but mostly left hooks because Lawrence was left handed. Then Lawrence demanded for us to come over and get a lick in. Mark quickly ran over and gave "Joe the Crier" a nice combo, one-two to the face.

Then it was my turn to exert a taste of revenge. I slowly approached the "God of the Alley"....

I hit him with all the strength that one finger could muster; I gently tapped Joe on the shoulder. Cousin Lawrence demanded that I hit him again. This time with a lot more purpose (hate). I hit "Joe the Crier" again with two fingers of absolute power... My mind racing that he would return the favor when my cousins were not around...

I then became more afraid of my Cousin Lawrence's anger and disappointment rather than the fear of the bully, **I then gave "Joe the Crier" a strong left jab. It felt so exhilarating, it felt so exhilarating.**

At that moment my cousin Lawrence delivered a left hook to my chest for being scared of the bully.

He then delivered his final left hook to "Joe the Crier". We never saw the bully again...

"OVERCOME" Words for YOU

> "If you demonstrate courage in front of your children, then they will carry courage away from you"
>
> On that same accord...
>
> "If you demonstrated anger / hate in front of your children, then they will carry anger / hate away from you."

Achievement;
Has more to do with

⬇

Believement
More than anything else...

No Excuses...Produces...

The FIRE

I remember the time our apartment was burned completely to the ground... The fire was so hot that the top floor of the apartment building collapsed onto the bottom floor... Although no one was hurt or injured in the fire...I was crushed, because I lost my new pair of tennis shoes. My mother realized how hurt I was... She tried to comfort me by promising that she would get me another pair. Our family had just got on our feet with our bills. It was a tremendous setback...

As a youngster I viewed this as a devastating setback because we lost everything... Today, as a Man I must confess that "THE FIRE" was not a setback but "The Fire" was a setup... The fire made us sit up and take notice of one another. We had family, we had friends, and we had each other. Some of you may need to take notice of the setup in your life. It's time for you to sit up and take notice of family and friends...it's time for you to take notice of your direction.

Well, as the story goes...I waited for the fire department to leave the dangerous scene so that I could go find my tennis shoes...My mother warned me to not go into the still smoking, water soaked ashes...But something was tugging on me, pulling at my curiosity to go find the shoes. So, without anyone's knowledge under the warning tape I went...

After carefully stepping, crawling, and sifting through burnt furniture, melted appliances, and other water soaked rubble it seemed all was lost...Then I came upon my mother's dresser. It was charred to the core. I began to cry... I cried because my Mom had been so proud of her bedroom furniture.

I then tugged on one of the drawers and gently pulled it open... and there inside the drawer was my Mom's Bible. The drawer also contained birth certificates, and other important papers...As I removed the items from the charred dresser, the dresser fell apart... The Bible was not touched by the fire...

Although I ventured that day into a place that my mother didn't want me to go, I found God's word that day…I found her Bible, and other important papers. If you haven't found Jesus yet, it's never too late… Have you ever ventured into a place that you were not supposed to go. Hello…You can find him in places that you shouldn't go. He's watching and waiting on you…

That untouched Bible was enough for me to start believing that day…I was saved from a butt whooping that day because I discovered HIS WORD. It's time for you to discover his word also. Jesus will save you today…He can find you in the most deserted place in your world. Call on him to save you. All may seem to be lost in your world… but Jesus will save you…

"OVERCOME" Words for YOU

"Growing Periods"... Teachers

Teachers are coaches and coaches are teachers. Coach's must scout, watch game films, practice offense and build defensive skills with the understanding of what it takes to win. As teachers we must also do due diligence in preparation to win the student. We must scout the students, study the strengths, weaknesses, and tendencies… Teachers cannot be simple providers of information. We must provide an uncluttered vision in the midst of a raging storm of tragedy. We must understand the students we are educating…If we fail to discover the strengths, weaknesses, tendencies of the student. We lose the game before the game has even began. Teachers must first devise an offensive and a defensive game plan for success. Not a plan by attacking the students, but a plan to combat anger, fear, insecurity, and low self-esteem by demonstrating understanding, tolerance, resilience, and determination to insure success.

Teachers must discover the sparkle that is deeply hiding behind the sty. "If we grow the *SPARKLE*, the *STY* will **_eventually_** disappear, but if we only treat the STY…the SPARKLE will **_never_** be discovered." Growth and discovery of the sparkle makes teaching easier, more gratifying, and more satisfying. Many struggling teachers believe teachers should be tougher on students to prepare them for the real world. This style allows teachers to excuse themselves of tolerance of silliness, laughter, or immaturity. This approach tend to justify (in their mind) and allow teachers off the hook of truly educating the student. Successful teachers are good teachers of their specialty, and great teachers of life. Great teachers are challenging, disciplined, organized and are not fearful of positive relationships with students.

"We must refuse to allow distracted students create a distracted teaching". Struggling teachers can be just as challenging, disciplined, and as organized, but seem to fear the positive relationships <u>students need for success</u>. They allow distracted students to create distracted teaching.

If *GROWING PERIODS are not acknowledged,* inflexibility, PERSONAL STANDards, lack of nurturing skill, or simply not understanding the true responsibility of teaching often will get in the way of student success. High expectation combined with low or poor relationships is a disaster for success. Everyone has *GROWING PERIODS*...a time in which they are learning, maturing, improving decision making skills, but also failing to make good choices making mistakes. *GROWING PERIODS ARE NEEDED...*
A first grader should not be treated as a 3rd or 4th grader... At risk students will struggle to meet expectation of teachers with poor connecting skills. Rookies are not treated like veterans. First year teachers do not have the experience of veteran teachers thus expectations are different. New mothers will not make the sound decisions of grandmothers.
    GROWING PERIODS ARE NEEDED...

I'm positive the key to teaching students is not treating them as if life has already dealt them a bitter pill...

Adults have regretful memories from their youth, as they approach their thirties, forties, or fifties (a growing period was needed to acknowledge that past moment in time)...

GROWING PERIOD are needed as we realize mistakes, poor decisions, and silliness is normal. We then can discover the SPARKLE deeply hiding behind the Sty. Once recognized, we will find it easy to say ***"Wow, you are very smart for your age young lady or young fella."*** Expectations of middle school and high school students to always make mature decisions are unreasonable. PERSONAL STANDards, lack of patience, and not seeking positive relationships may be the CAUSE and AFFECT of low performance, not the student.

  Teachers....Don't shrug or judge 'em...
  It's okay to bug 'em or even hug 'em...

"OVERCOME" Words for YOU

The Crossing Tree

I think I've found the purpose of my life
To document the pain, agony,
Of those sacrificed

The purpose, the world and all the need to see
The sacrifice of the one nailed to the
"Crossing Tree"

The Crossing Tree saves us all from a
World of Sin
The gift of eternal life, can you imagine

A world where no one cares
Turns at an unnatural pace
A world of compassion and generosity
The pace he chased

"Father, why has thou forsaken me",
His final Cry"
Three days later God, lifted his Son
Up for his final ride high through the sky

For those who are lost or shut out,
My pen will be remember your voice
The voice of compassion,
My purpose was God's choice

So my commitment forever
Never to forget his Face
And remind the world of the
"Greatness of his Grace"

Wow, Nothing needs to be said to introduce
Death Bed

What would you say if today was judgement day?
Who would you miss? Would it be your first kiss?

Who would you write?
The purchaser of your first Bike

Who would you want to see?
The one that served the cool sweet tea

Who would you text?
The one with whom you could connect

Laying in your death bed,
Who would you cry for?
The one that would trade places,
that cared even more

Who would cry for you?
The one that gave birth and know you are true

What book would you want to read?
Maybe the Bible or book on "How to Succeed?

What would your friends say?
You were a good person, we wish you could stay

What would you sister feel?
Agony and depression enough to wish for your ordeal

"OVERCOME" Words for YOU

What would your brother do?
Punch the wall, get drunk, and end it too?

Whats going on in your best friends mind?
We had a great friendship
So many good times, good times, short time?

What about the old lady across the street?
She witnessed my growing pains at her feet

She always yell to me "Boy! Get out of the road"
I wish to hear her voice today
But that road is about to closed

What about my Mom's boyfriend?
I rejected him because he tried to move in

What about my first grade teacher
What would she say?
Does she still have that picture I drew?
My first crush revealed that day.

Some twisted soul posted my picture
on social media to say
"Get Well, Go to Hell! Lets fight again today!
No time, Not enough time, Damn, no way!

My time left on earth is quickly ticking
I can't get distracted with hate.
I must think about the ones I love
and hope for the Pearly Gates!

I must now live each moment to its fullest,
And forget about the burdens of the past.
I must spend my final moments on earth, dreaming
and holding, my love one's last

What do I do now?
My dreams are coming to an end.
My eyes closed
Yet, I'm still seeing faces of family and friends.

Oh God! I just need another chance
A change in me will me made.
I need more time to repair a Man in disaray

Spending my last moments wisely,
Dreaming of family and friends
I wish I would have done that sooner.
Why did I wait until the end?

I've seen and lived more today,
Than I have in twenty years
At least I will die with family,
Friends and happy tears

Darkness soon arrived,
My heart slowed to a final beat.
My last breath taken, I felt a tag on my feet.

....
....
....

"OVERCOME" Words for YOU

A jolt to my heart electrified my eyes
Someone was trying to bring me back alive.

Don't let go, don't let go was the cry.
Did I cheat death? Or was it just a disguise?

I heard three voices, a combination of three
Each softly whispering,
Giving a valant effort to save me

The three voices, God, my Grandmother,
and my Mother, were voices of gold.
Their beautiful trio awakened my SOUL

I survived it seems. Was this a miracle or a dream?
Am I going to make it! Oh God please don't fake it

There was happiness around the room
My death bed still surrounded, none left to soon.

I have my life back now, not old but NEW
My life dedicated to family and friends
And especially that quartet too.

I ran to the old lady that lives across the street.
Thank you! Thank you! I said
As I began messaged her tired feet.

Before I left, I grabbed her broom
I swept the porch, sidewallk and even the street

The same street where I always played,
She yelled again…her voice sounded so sweet.

I then raced to see the purchaser of my first bike.
"Please take a picture with me, I think we look alike??? I I I I I I think we look alike!!!

There on the porch my grandmother sits
I remember her distinct hands and her sweet tea
Her only request was; boy get some ice, share some time, and for me to be a good me

My tender Mom, she would have died for me
Trading places so clear and true
Her sacrifices for me and my brothers
I dedicated my RENEWED life too

She smiled as I began to read the Bible
I shared the glory with my friends.
I then hugged my sisters and brothers
And promised to never leave them again

I searched for the old boyfriend of my Mom's
Selfishness had made me take a immature stand
I will give my first born his name
because he wanted me to be a strong MAN

My first crush reveald during my early years
I then raced to her class with excitement and tears.

The crush now cemented to her face with joy.
Oh God!She screamed!
"Good to see you standing boy!"

"OVERCOME" Words for YOU

The fighting guy that posted the twisted thought
Was hard to find.
So I posted his picture on the internet
Explaining he was a friend of mine

A $500 reward for a phone call or to come and see
I desperately need to speak with him,
To repair both him and me.

He called, we laughed, he said I was a fool.
But after that conversation I had a great feeling
knowing that we were again cool.

I whispered "What a great life I have"
My Mom quickly interrupted and then sternly said
"Never forget the promise you made on your DEATHBED"

....

"You don't have to be a professional writer to write life changing words"...
Words from the heart more powerful than any other words...

"Sometimes you must retire to your new Life". Retire to a new commitment, retire to a new Happiness, retire to a new Greatness, retire to explore God's new purpose for you...Rewarded...

Believe in Yourself !

Pride will get you KILLED
Not all pride is good pride

You Get, what you Give!

"The Greatest Compliment you can receive...
Who Raised That Boy/Girl?"
"I would like to meet your Mother and Grandmother"

"The Greatest Person I ever met was my Mother's Mother"

Good Songs are always too short...
I wish they could last forever...
I guess they do in our hearts"

"OVERCOME" Words for YOU

"Wear your tragedies As armor, not shackles"
This poster made a lot sense to me.

You may not have a Father growing up, but your kids can have one. Don't Leave 'em!!!

"I enjoy Reading, I read people everyday...When you learn to read your students, that's when the real teaching starts"...

Tragedy and Disappointment

Bad things happen to everyone. Tragedy and disappointment is as natural as happiness and success.

"If you hang in there you can sweat out feverish disappointment and soon began to feel better.

Days turn into weeks, weeks turn into months, and months turn into years.

Tragic moments provide opportunities for personal growth and a more grounded you."

"Don't Take It Personal"

"OVERCOME" Words for YOU

Fourth and Inches

I remember this story of a little boy...
The boy stepped on the scale to get his weight and height measurement. All the boys were getting their yearly physicals that were required to participate in athletics.

As the boy step to the scale the Athletic Trainer notice the boy had grown a bit and made the comment, **"Young Man, it looks like you've grown a bit."** As the trainer lifted the head stand to begin to measure the boy's height, the boy silently dismissed the possibility that he had grown or gotten taller. He felt he was still and always would be a pimpled face runt in his mind. All he had done all summer was ride a skate board to escape intrusions. The boy had always been short, insecure, and thinly built.

After the measurement the trainer turned to the young boy and said, **"Son, you've grown about 4 inches over the summer".** FOUR! FOUR! FOUR! FOUR!!! **Thundered through his mind, heart and soul at that very moment...**
He began sweating, hyperventilating and worrying for reasons unknown to the trainer.

As his palms became sweaty his mind raced back to a tragic day three months earlier... a day he was mighty low... mighty depressed... mighty confused...and mighty angry...
The boy had made promises that he now must keep since it seemed his prayer had been answered.

That day had started normal; the boy was watching the big guys play basketball. He asks them if he could play but they refused, laughing and mock his nappy uncombed hair.
 "Get your little #!% out of here punk with your nappy #@% hair...
So he stood on the side watching intently wishing that he could play. The never let him...

"He waited for the Sun to go home, so everyone else would be gone. He would practice and play alone in darkness, then his light would began to shine"

The court didn't have a night light; he always practiced alone in darkness so no one would be there to bother him. However, on this day that changed. Just before the sun left, the guys strangely yelled Come on, come join the fun.

This is what the boy's heart heard;
"Come play with us...you're one of us now...We will never call you names again,...We want you to be around us...We are your friends...We accept you!!!

"OVERCOME" Words for YOU

This is actually what they said;
"Hey little punk, we need another player, come on and don't mess up".

Evidently, some of the other players had left so another player was needed to play. The boy was grateful for the invite though. He was so excited to play, the boy ran up and down the court at least a hundred times never touching the ball, and playing defense on everyone, his own team and the other team. It didn't matter that they never pass the ball to him. He was just happy to be one of the accepted boys. The boy was open every time down the court because no one guarded him. He really didn't care because he was finally being accepted...

Then it happened...the moment forever etched in the boy's mind. His newly formed friends said, "Hey little Man, catch and shoot this ball...The boy (little Man, yea) was so excited, for the first time the guys was talking directly to him, not at him, encouraging him to shoot the ball. This moment did wonders immediately to his self-esteem, finally being accepted and a part of the group.

So as pass floated to his waiting hands, it was perfect...He caught the basketball with the carefulness of a brain surgeon. He wasn't about to ruin this moment by missing or fumbling the ball. Everyone began to yell Shoot it, Shoot it!!! He couldn't believe the encouragement his ears were receiving. As he began to shoot the ball, the boy noticed everyone smiling and so happy for him to shoot. This was his "Jordan moment". As the boy began to shoot the ball,

Tragedy struck. A big guy ran from behind him and blocked his shot...

Little Man (the boy) never saw him...The big guy was hiding the whole time...
The big guy hit the ball so hard it slammed into the boy's ear. He dropped to the ground in shock, anguish and heartbroken as everyone laughed ....*as everyone laughed........*
"Get up! You little piece of #$&# !" ...
The boy's lifeless body refused to move. The only movement was from tears running away from the boy's wounded eyes.

That very moment had been a set up to humiliate him from the start. As darkness began to shine on the basketball court, the boy found himself all alone.

He was left alone with his humiliation, depression, embarrassment, and rejection from the tragic "Jordan moment." He hated those boys for what they had done to him that day. As the boy contemplated how to relieve such brutal anguish, he remembered something his Grandmother would always do in moments like this.

She would just sing out "Oh Lord, Oh Lord"
The boy's Grandmother always would do a singing pray in her back room at night before going to bed. So he (the boy) began to mimic the

greatest person he ever met... His Mother's Mother...then he began to sing like her....

Oh Lord... Oh Lord... Oh Lord... then he began to speak...Please help me today...I'm just tired Lord...

The Boy gave God a whole list of I'm tired request...

-tired of the big boys not allowing me to play basketball on the courts...

-tired of being picked on...

-tired of walking the halls in fear of the bullies...

-tired of seeing my Mother struggle with a hurt back...

-tired of the unfair hand my Brother was dealt...please trade me, why him not me!

-tired of Moms boyfriends...

-tired of smelling cigarette smoke in my clothes

-just tired of life's struggles

He asks God to give him four inches in height because at the time he was just tired;

"If you could just grant me four inches in height the boy asked. He promised to be a good person the rest of my life. He promised to never throw rocks or eggs at cars again. He repeated his promise to be a good person and when people looked into his eyes they would find kindness and compassion and see the glory of God's unselfish love. After that night, the boy continued to ride his skateboard the remainder of the summer. As a matter of fact three months later he rode his skateboard to the high school on get a free Physicals Day". As the boy approached the scale his soul was awakened once again... **"Young Man, it looks like you've grown a bit."**

I believed that if I became taller it would eliminate most of the frustration that I was facing. The four inches brought a change in my life. The bullying stopped...I began to walk the hall without fear...I became stronger, taller, and able to lift my Brother and push him around town...No man ever hit my Mom again!

I honored all my promises and commitments. I received a scholarship to play college basketball, graduated, got married, became more than just a coach, raised my family, but more importantly became the Man my Mother and Grandmother planted in me.

"OVERCOME" Words for YOU

FOUR! FOUR! FOUR! FOUR!

"Thundered through My mind, my heart, And my soul At that very moment"

> "As you become a parent it is so important to allow your children to fix what was damaged in you as a child"

Today's messages

"If we forget those that were lost... Then we really lose those we remember"

"OVERCOME" Words for YOU

"I NEVER COUNTED MY WINS OR LOSES BUT I REMEMBER EVERY VICTORY"

WHAT IS POPULAR IS NOT ALWAYS RIGHT
WHAT IS RIGHT IS NOT ALWAYS POPULAR
(This sign has hung in my office for over twenty years)

"As I grew, my storming attitude was often Misunderstood, because my speech was difficult But as I mature, my life will have clearer skies because the storms will have moved on"…

Teach every day!!!
Reach every day!!!
Motivate every day!!!

I know people that do this every day... The fact you may be a custodian, teacher's aide, cashier, cook, salesman, student, part-time worker, whatever the position should not be a hindrance to your passion of helping others...

Your position is not important; you can make a difference... Save a life...Be prepared to teach, reach, and motivate every day...

"It's your Passion not your Position"

"TO COACH OR TEACH
IS THE GREATEST POSITION I WAS TOLD.

TO COACH, TO TEACH, TO MOTIVATE

A BALANCED MAN OR WOMEN MUST UNFOLD"

"OVERCOME" Words for YOU

Imperfect But Perfect

She was not perfect
But she was perfect for me
I've been blessed with the best imperfect
Mother there could ever be

Her smile brings life to a dead phone
Her spirit would bring calmness
To a heavy metal song

The alphabet don't contain enough
letters from A to Z
I need a thousand more letters
To express what she did for me

Not many souls walk the earth in
perfect soles
God the only one that most of us knows

So never be distracted
Because perfection is not the real key
Love, kindness, and generosity
Were the keys she gave me

Never in my life will I ever feel cheated
To give abundantly without
expectations is what most people needed

She taught me that lesson well
A lesson she constantly lived,
She didn't have to tell

I can never repay that Mom of mine,
For my life, my brothers, my family,
and her time

Imperfection is Perfection in a world of
illusions
She surrendered her all,
So we would avoid the confusion

God please blessed her once she's
finished and her time to come home
We all must follow her someday
To be judge by our own song

Lord, I know you already understand
You're getting the best imperfect
But perfect Mom of any Man

"OVERCOME" Words for YOU

Mr. E on Tragic Moments

Tragic Moments happen to everyone...

MOVING ON does not mean that you're not hurt, or that you didn't love the lost one.

Tragedy is personal, but NOT A PERSONAL ATTACK.
Don't take it Personal...
Cry ⟹ Survive ⟹ Revive
Then THRIVE

"The plan was to commit the crime and do the time and enjoy every sunrise in prison. I even thanked God for helping me with the ease of the decision."
Excerpt from "The Punch"...

WHERE'S MY MOM?
NO TIME IN SPACE OR SPACE IN TIME
SPACE, TIME, I'VE LOST MY MIND

WhereisMyMom?Shewassickatthetime.AmIlosingmymind?IgottofindNo.Never,isshelost.Searchandfindmygreatestboss.Myheadisspinningtoseemyfirstgirl.Theearthstoppedspinningandsodidmyworld.Itseemstobe _nospaceintimeortimeinspace_, whatdoIdonowshe'sgonewithoutatrace..I'mconfusedandalonenowIdon'tunderstand.Nochoicenow,IgottobetheManshepланned?Breathe, breathe…take a deep breath

....

Finally, there she is now I can see
Her spirit was there the whole time,
within me!

Look in the mirror, smile and give a toast.
I will never leave you; I'm your Mama
Angel not a Ghost.

"OVERCOME" Words for YOU

ONE

It only takes 1 to change a life
It only takes 1 break to change a life
It only takes 1 pet to change a life
It only takes 1 hero to change a life
It only takes 1 to care to change a life
Your turn to finish this...
It only takes 1 mistake to change a life

It only takes 1_____

It only takes 1_____

It only takes 1_____

It only takes 1_____

We must demonstrate compassion for others... It's a STRENGTH...

"The Struggle"
You're not a victim!!!
You're not a Lie!!!
You're a Fact!!!
You're Blessed!!!

**The word
INSIGNIFICANT
Should forever be removed
From the English
Language!!!**

Everyone Matters!

"OVERCOME" Words for YOU

Story Time
The Stop Sign

This sign reminds me of a time when I was a troubled teen, running around doing stupid things.

My friends (my boys) and I decided to have a contest on the best decorated bedroom. We would go around town collect items to use to decorate our bedrooms. We would collect things such as stop signs, yield signs, constructions lights, anything that would look good on the walls of our rooms. Nothing was off limits as long as it would fit on your wall. Business signs, flashing warning lights, and even beer signs were in danger of being collected for Wall of Fame material.

After finishing my room, which I describe as a master piece, my thoughts were of winning the bet. **The winner would get to wear the nice silk shirt to the next house party. We shared and rotated that shirt regularly.** My room had a black net stretched under the purple light, with trinkets and other objects gently place to provide the full effect of the purple light. On the wall was a huge stop sign that I borrowed from one of the local corners. Also hanging from corner to the other corner was a multi-colored paper Mache chain that glowed in the dark and shined brilliantly under the purple haze from the light. My friends had pretty much the same type of theme for their rooms, but mine was the best in my opinion.

Well, my Mom came home to discover the huge Stop sign hanging on my wall and gently ask me to take it back... Well that's not exactly how she asked me...as a matter of fact she said,

"Boy, get your butt in here and get this damn sign out of here. What's wrong with you? Do you want to get someone killed? Put that Stop sign back, take it back right now".

Yes Mama I replied, but the judges (my friends) of the contest still hadn't judged my room. I couldn't remove my winning decoration before the judges had seen the winning master piece. I did not return the sign like my mother had demanded of me.

A few days later my mother drove through that same intersection where I had removed the stop sign. The other car was speeding and failed to stop (because the sign was still missing) narrowly missed hitting my mother's car. My mother could have been killed. My Mom driving the old brown Delta 88 didn't know of the near miss accident. But we witness the incident. My heart skipped a couple of beats at that moment.

I raced home before my mom could get home to take the stop sign down. If my Mother would've gotten home to see the Stop sign still hanging on my wall, I would not be recognizable for a few days. She would let my whooping's add up before I'd get the big one. I immediately returned the sign to the corner pole.

Wow, as I think about that day, sometimes you don't realize how your actions affect others. I never forgot the lesson and continue to look at life through the eyes of others ever since…

It was a **BLESSING** that my mother didn't get seriously hurt that day. My life would have led to a **DEAD END** because of the guilt of stealing a sign that led to my mom's accident or maybe her death. I needed to **STOP** being stupid and become aware of how my actions affect others…

"OVERCOME" Words for YOU

Your Page

"The power behind me is greater than the problem in front of me."

Serve Your Purpose

"If you're serving your purpose, God will move obstacles out of your way or move you...

You must be willing to move, you can't allow your pride to nail you to the ground...

God may need you to fly...You may be needed somewhere else"

Coach Etheridge

"It's a Great Day to Be Alive"

His long lashes attempted
To hide
The hopelessness of life, inside his eyes,
But a patient one
Will look and
Discover inside the eye
The deep hidden sparkle lurking
Behind the sty
Excerpt from "Find the Sparkle"

....

As she look at me, her mind sometimes confused and in a daze,
The end IS near.

I had to convince her at that exact moment

That her unknown Father WAS missing out on her GREATNESS

She WAS only missing out on his LATENESS
You're Great, He's Late
I SHOUTED TO HER WORLD!

"The Sledge Hammer"

The Sledge Hammer is used to drive an obstacle into an unwilling surface. It is also used to exert maximum power for maximum results.

One of my favorite motivational quotes from a dear friend and masterful coach: He would say *"Sometimes you have to kill a Gnat with a sledge hammer"*-Harry Miller- **There will be times when you must use more force than required. There will be times when we must do more than what's required. We would remind our players to...**
Wear your tragedies as armor not shackles...

HM

Keys to a Good Speaker

It's easy to speak to Young People
-Keys to a Good Speaker:
-Know Yourself
-Know Your Subject
-Know Your Audience
Admit that....
...YOU DON'TKNOW EVERYTHING
Young people recognize a fake...

"OVERCOME" Words for YOU

Family or Partners

It seems like none of my partners are partners no more...

Acting like they're down with me, friends they pretend to be because of some color or hood you see...

*But in the end they will regret their decisions to turn their back on me...
A lottery winner I see I see
Raise my family in*

HONESTY

Mind your own business because yours is not in order. Sometimes students refuse to focus on themselves to find flaws. So they focus and speak negatively of others to distract from their own faults.
No Sir, Not Today!!!

That's What Daddy's Do!!!

Message for Daddy's and Fathers...
Tell the devil today...right now! I rebuke you!
You can't have my relationship with my wife...
You can't have my relationship with my children...
You cannot have my relationship with my family...
You cannot have my relationship with God...
Get out!!!...
I'm about to do something special and I will not allow you to distract the greatness that is to become...
In Jesus name, in Jesus name I claim Amen...

Down but Never Out because of My

_____

Write the name here

Which Super Hero is the Greatest __*Crime Fighter?*__
...Superman?...Batman?
...Spider Man?...Captain America?
....
A Father in the Home

**"It's not the Drugs that's messing me up.
It's My Decisions that lessening me up.
Sometimes my Pops think I don't understand, but I'm working to become a better man."
My mind is more complex and powerful than any Drug...**

Do You Know CPR?

It's like the ambulance driver that was giving CPR to the victim in the car wreck...He was working hard to save the person's life...After a while he felt it was a hopeless case, too much damage had been done...As he was about to give up, a stranger approached and told him that he knew CPR as well... He said it's no use Sir...it's too late...

The stranger then said "let me give it a try"... He looked at the stranger as he started his version of CPR; the stranger started praying...

You see my CPR is CHRIST'S POWER REVEALED...
"Jesus Christ has awesome Power and can be revealed through prayer" That's the CPR you need today...

Just like Jesus saved that young man I know he will save you today...He is an expert in saving the lost...In the mist of your darkness he will provide light... He will lift your spirits, rejuvenate your heart, and clear your mind...He can bring the dead back to life...Lazarus was dead...but Jesus gave him a shot of the living blood...

We must start our CPR class today...Christ's Power Revealed thru prayer...If you think you are having a heart attack, or shortness of breath, or shortness of time in a troubled marriage. You better believe in CPR...

IF you or someone you know has lost their will to LIVE, LOVE, or LAUGH. You better believe in CPR... If your mother, grandmother can't control your attitude or spirit... You better believe in CPR... If your rent, car payment, or transmission is slipping and the mechanic won't accept post- dated checks... You better believe in CPR... CPR is CHRIST'S POWER REVEALED...

Excerpt from the Speech..."Forgive to Live"

"OVERCOME" Words for YOU

The Wheel Chair

The Man mysteriously left the unknown scene
Slightly before the Boy's first Dream

The early birth produced a light weight Baby
The unknown Man to be more crippled maybe

The Man never drinking a Fathers taste
Not ever knowing of or ever seeing his Boy's face

The Boy's life full of steep peaks and deep valleys
The mystery Man life deep in shadowy alleys

Because neither knew of the other, it's hard to complain
The double unknown is hard to explain

The Boy's biggest regret is "I remember when"
The unknown Mans regret
Not knowing his start was the end

Family, friends and sports, events of all kind
The unknown Man <u>missing</u>
The pleasures of the boys mind

A lottery ticket his life was loaded with Joy
The Unknown Man missed out on the riches of his Boy

Soon the wheel chair crowned Man enlightened the World
The Man path missed out on **God's Rolling Pearl**

The wheel chair birthed a tremendous Man
Because the GREATEST FATHER had a better PLAN
"Tragic Moments Can Fuel a Lifetime of Bitterness or Greatness"

Forty-Three Kicks

My Brother kicked me in the butt 43 times one day in front of my friends (My Boys). I was at the courts showing off with my friends cursing and trying to be accepted. I cursed at him. I called him a #$%#%$^&...

Then he kicked me...I glanced at my boys, they laughed a little, then looked at me...I was embarrassed; I was in front of my boys so I said it again and again...
Every time I said it, he would kick me...Each kick hurt...After being kicked forty three times (my boys did a good job counting each kick out loud) I ran home with tears running away from my eyes.

My Brother never told my Mother...He simply stated to me later that night..."Mama didn't raise us like that"...

       I never curse him again...
       Thanks Bro, I love you...JDK...

Joel Darnell Kindred

Story Time
The Little Voice

Women, leave me alone! I know how to drive! I have the right away....

You need to slow down there are cars speeding over there

...The traffic over there must yield! Leave me alone, I can drive....

....I then heard **a little voice** whispering *"you better listen to your wife"*

...the voice sounded familiar

...it sounded like my grandmother, my mom, or voice from God

...or a combination of all of them

...I slammed on the brakes to slow the car to a stop

...I'm thankful, I stopped car

....a ½ second later, a truck speeding at 95mph missed our car by about 2 inches...

...our car swayed, shook, and vibrated because of near miss ...

....my life flashed before my eyes...

...I saw visions that had occurred at different moments in my life, all in that split second

...including a vision of

...My mother at my funeral....

...My grandmother's crying...

...My family asking God why...

...I began to cry...

...then I began to chase the truck on a death chase...

...then my wife screamed at me to stop...

....I stopped the car...

....We cried....We cried...

I listen now...now I listen...

You would not be reading this book ...

If I didn't stop to listen to that voice...tears...

"OVERCOME" Words for YOU

"My Past was a Struggle,
But Still
My Dreams,
My Life,
My Future,
My Hope,
Points to GREATNESS"

"Sometimes accidents make Life unfair,
This made anger grab ahold of me.
I now realize that person was a stranger.
The accident was meant to be because

Now I know the real **ME**"

Get Busy Not Dizzy

OBK

Find Your Fuel

I FOUND MINE IN TEMPLE TEXAS

"OVERCOME" Words for YOU

"The Harder You Work, The Luckier You Get"

CONTROL YOUR EMOTIONS OR YOUR EMOTIONS WILL CONTROL YOU!!!

Successful Marriage
I was talking to a friend the other day and he said something startling;
The Key to a successful happy wife was <u>The Three Step Plan</u>;
1) Treat her like a Princess...
2) Do anything for her...
3) See 1 and 2...

Wow, What a Great Message...

He was a Great Father also...

TP

"I just want to improve my chances"

Fa_r_ther Needed

A Boy without a Father
Will search quick and fast
To find the Man that did not last...

He will run, hustle, and find the game
To replace the lost fathers crime,
He'll never be the same.

The Boy will accept fast money
and a dead end plan
Because he didn't have his #1 fan
To help him refuse temptation,
and to withstand

Today I will evaluate my own plan
Thanks Mom, I understand

Your voice now clear, I hear your advice,
Better choices are on the way because
I finally understand your sacrifice,,,

"OVERCOME" Words for YOU

Believe in Yourself

Or you will always Leave Yourself

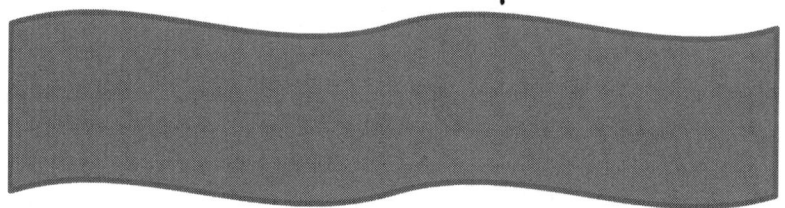

"A HANDSHAKE IS LIKE A FINGER PRINT.

IT WILL TELL OTHERS WHAT'S INSIDE OF YOU..."

(<u>firm</u>...thumb skin to thumb skin...<u>firm</u>)

Simple Thoughts from a simple Man.
Using simple lines in a complex time...

GRIT GRIT **GRIT**
GRIT
GRIT GRIT **GRIT**
GRIT

Don't Ever Give Up & Don't Ever Quit!!!

MT

The Punch

I saw him punch my Mom
His aim was straight.
Her face shattered, receiving a punch from a drunken Heavyweight.

My life changed that day
To God I confessed and prayed.
He was wrong; I'm going to kill him
Was the prayer that stayed

The plan was to commit the crime and do the time then enjoy every sunrise in prison.
I even thanked God for helping me
With the ease of the decision

He sucker-punched her,
I swore revenge that day
And every between day
Several years later came my opportunity to repay.

I had carried revenge for a solid ten
Never forgetting her crushed jaw
I was much older now,
Pretending to be a better me, but
"<u>SHE ATE FOOD THROUGH A STRAW!</u>"

Anger seething, the whole damn time
Surprised I didn't have high blood pressure
Or a stoke of some kind

He was in the hospital
My Mom requested of me to see.
See the Man that put her down,
I took my knife with me.

She said, get a report, and show respect
Please pray for his health.
Sure Mom I said as I hastily left,
Wondering should I use my knife, or my belt.

I couldn't get the image out of my mind.
He dropped her with malice,
I can't erase that time.

I rushed to the hospital to end his fate.
I rushed to face the one responsible for my hate.

My pain never went away, it was always there.
My heart and mind racing with anger,
In deep need of repair.

I prayed and confessed to God long ago,
"I will get that Joker this I know."

I eased to the 4th floor,
to send him to a six foot pit.
Looking around, I eased through the door
I didn't give a blip.

"OVERCOME" Words for YOU

It seemed like a lifetime
Of carrying this burden around
Now is the time for this clown to go down.

"John I yelled, look and see.
Do you remember the night?
You beat my Mom and me"

Today is the **DAY**, I had prayed and prayed.
Thank you God! It's my time to repay.

His head slowly began to rise.
Slow enough for me to see his lifeless eyes.
Hey Man, it's me it's me. Can't you see!!!
My lifetime burden I got to set free…

He was old and gray,
His face shriveled and over tanned.
So thin, so frail, so weak,
He wasn't the same Man.

Who are you he then slowly asks?
"Man, it's time to repay
And I don't accept cash!!!

Who are you? He asks again, I leaned in…
Damn, the nurse rush in!

Does he remember you? The nurse softly asks,
She sounded caring and very nice.
<u>**"He doesn't recognize many, his mind was sacrificed.**</u>

What, Why, What, When, Is this what it seems?
This is not the same guy
That destroyed our dreams.

Alzheimer's disease had ravaged his brain,
So the fact he didn't remember me
Became the other agonizing pain

"God this is not fair, he needs to see my face
My wrinkles of burden are easy to trace."

I can't hurt a man that doesn't understand,
That death was in close brush.
Alzheimer's hit him in the head
But it's my head that's crushed.

A lost old man barely able to stand,
He just cheated his death song.
But why do I feel cheated,
Why did I carry hate for so long!?!

Angrily, I phoned my Mom to explain the situation.
Strangely she said *forgive Him son, forgive him or it will change your destination…*
…breathe…breathe…

I understood the importance of obeying her request.
Mom's never lead their children astray,
Moms always know best.

"OVERCOME" Words for YOU

<u>She understood my burden,</u>
<u>She planned this all along</u>.
"You need to let go of that burden Son,
And then please come home."

Damn…Damn…I said it twice…
No need to follow through
Or make that sacrifice
My family survived, and I have a great life…

He looked old and frail
Today was his lucky day
Hey Man, I forgive you,
My voice quivered and struggled to say.

So at that moment again I said
"Hey Man; I forgive you for what you did."
A voice from God whispered in my ear…
"I took care of it."

"Message"

As a young coach, the most important words ever spoken to me was this quote.

> "Coach,
>
> We can't help them if they're not here"
>
> We can't run them off"
>
> Bob McQueen

Cowards Strike Women!

"If you feel the need to strike her, then leave her"

Don't fight, just do what's Right

A BOY that DISRESPECTS GIRLS *will become*... A MAN that will DISRESPECT WOMEN!

Start Changing Now A Little Each Day...

Why do you want people to see your EXCUSE? You should want people to see your USE"
I SHOUTED TO HIS WORLD!

We must demonstrate compassion for others...It is Strength...

I forget the death days of loved ones...

BUT
I will never forget...
I will always REMEMBER their living days...

God Bless You!

Nearsighted

Nearsighted vision is often distorted vision because GREATNESS is hard to recognize when the view is magnified to see imperfections.

Sometimes you can be too close to someone to appreciate their GREATNESS.

Sometimes you must back off, backup, or step away to appreciate their path, what they've overcome, the person they are now...

Hello my friend,

    We may not always get to see the finished product of our effort. However, the troubled kid will never forget you or what you've done for them. This book is to say thank you and to offer you continued motivation to make a difference.

My purpose is for the troubled kids or tough students reading these pages that you realize help is on the way. Hang in there; just hold on, Survive, Revive, and Thrive...

My goodness, everyone makes mistakes...It's not a life sentence to make a mistake or to be a troubled young kid. Don't be judgmental, crushing, or unforgiving of yourself. You are important, you count, and you are you.

The word INSIGNIFICANT should forever be removed from the English Language!!! Everyone Matters!

Sincerely,
Bruce Etheridge

PS..."Nurture their wounds past their shackles"

You Don't Have To Be

You don't have to be a basketball player to play basketball...

You don't have to be a baseball player to hit a baseball...

You don't have to be a writer to write life changing words...

You don't have to be a fool to make foolish mistakes...

Thank God that

You don't have to be a praying man to ask for Forgiveness...but it helps...

On Step Fathers...

If you don't know your real Father or have a relationship with him, your Mom's boyfriend **MAY** the one... A man that will raise another man's child as his own is a Mountain of a man. "He is Special" Give him credit!!! Call him Daddy if he deserves it!!!
Step-Father or Real Father
WHO STEPPED OUT?   WHO STEPPED IN?
Don't run them off because of your own bitterness,
Your Mom deserves to be happy and grow old with companionship...

Coach, I want to be a Marine...
"Hold up Chief"
"You may want to be a Marine,
But you're training to be a Cub Scout!"

"It's time to grow up and fix your anger and attitude.
Fix your attitude!!!
Fix the issues that's getting in the way of your MARINE goal Chief."

"OVERCOME" Words for YOU

Comments

Your deliberate time for family has never gone un-noticed. Alexandra's poem (Thanksgiving Dessert) is an example of the impact you have made in the lives of youth in our family down thru the years.......... Thank you.

Great coach!!!

ANOTHER HIT! Says so much in such few words!

"The Punch" Pure Intensity!!!
INCREDIBLY inspiring and thought-provoking

DO YOUR THING, MR. E!!

Thank you Coach Etheridge. That is an awesome poem. I have watched you father all of your kids from the time I was a young man under your wings, all the way through my adulthood. I am most impressed with your strength, patience, wisdom, understanding, and unconditional love. You have been the ultimate and perfect role model to follow. You taught me well. God placed you in my path when I and my single mother needed you most. I will be forever grateful for your friendship. You are a true Guardian Angel! We love you!

Thank you coach, I'm honored to have been a life inspiration for you. Well done; I am impressed.

Bruce you're recognizing and walking in the grace & purpose God has created you to be is exceptional.

Looks great, man. You're gonna have a book soon!

So many truths...I wish the wounded child could have healed itself, but in this life all cannot be healed. Men who didn't have fathers themselves don't always know how to be fathers when they didn't have the nurturing themselves. We break generational curses...one generation at a time...thank God!

What a great gift! God blessed me with you in September of 1975, and he blessed me again today with your poem. I have shared about our Travis Mustang years with many coaches over the years. I told them about a great little point guard who turned into a great basketball coach. I also told them I taught you how to play Ping Pong!! Thanks for the memories!!

Awesome! Very deep, it is full of finding the man and maturing into a man. States what it takes to become a man when a man was not there to help you become one, but knowing you have to teach one when you have one.
Great tribute, Gone but not forgotten…

Wow, Death Bed is a Killer…my favorite…

Unbelievable Man! You knew what to send me…How? Why?

Thank you, I am crying thank you thank you thank you…

So inspirational, I need to "Shut up and Get Busy"!

Finally help for the single parent kid…Thanks Mr. E…

I WONDER IF YOU REALIZE WHAT YOU'VE DONE WITH THIS BOOK.

He heard, saw, and felt my heartbeat.

Finally, someone knows what to say to me

There is not enough room on here to say all the good things about you coach. And there is no way we can repay you for what you have done for me and everyone else. But I can say thank you coach. You will always be one of my heroes. We love you no matter what. A hero to me is someone that will give all they have without expecting anything in return. Much love Coach Bruce Etheridge…RG…

"Find a Hero in your World, and then become a Hero in their World"

"In love, 100 pennies do not equal a dollar"

Thanks to Carlos Salinas for your inspiring encouragement during this project. Your encouragement instilled my vision.

I BELIEVE

Every child born has a purpose in life. The purpose of the child may be yours to fulfill or his to accept. Are you afraid of not fulfilling or serving your purpose? Someone may be waiting on you to save them. Someone maybe searching for you because God has sent them on their purposeful mission to find you hug you save you from yourself. You may be someone that's turning a blind eye on your rescuer... The word INSIGNIFCANT should be removed from the English language...Everyone Matters...God Bless...

Bruce Etheridge

    I finally gained enough confidence to go to the side door of the house and knock. Tap, tap, and tap I tapped softly. My mind began racing with anticipation and fear, all at the same time. In those seconds before the door open my thoughts became questions again. What is he going to look like? Will I look like him? Is he tall, fat, thin, or small? Heck I don't care. I just need to see him!

    Is he going to be happy to see me? Wait, why has he not talked to me before? I've played in this street all the time. As a matter of fact, this kid on the mini bike could not be his son because his dad left a long time ago. Heck, I don't care; I just need to see my Dad...

"OVERCOME" Words for YOU

You are not responsible for your parents

BURDENS

Don't Judge them …
FIX YOURSELF !

Overcome Words of Encouragement and Speeches of Impact ©

Hey Superman Hey Wonder Women

As a child I remember the boys playing with their Superman action figures (toys)…I also remember the Girls would play with their "Wonder Woman" dolls…Boys played with action figures and girls played with dolls…

The truth is both boys and girls played with dolls and action figures. With visions of saving them in their world……Saving them from an abusive father, or an alcoholic mother, maybe a poverty stricken home, or even a drug infested home with constant fighting…

We dreamed of Superman or Wonder Woman to the rescue…Girls dreamed of "the "Girl Power" that Wonder Woman possessed to save them and to protect them…Boys dreamed of the super powers of Superman to "Protect and Serve" to leap tall buildings on a single bound…Today I say to you…

Neither Superman nor Wonder Woman Is Coming to Save You!

So many of you are looking around for someone to blame, there is no one to blame for your situation. Life is tough. It's tough for you, it was tough on your Mother, and it was tough on your Daddy, your grandmother, your older brother…Just ask them... Quit looking for someone to blame, or someone to save you. Neither Super Man nor Wonder Woman is coming… Life is tough so it's time for you to get tougher…

I know where Super Man and Wonder Women live… I know where they are, I know where they hide… I see them but you don't recognize them because they're in disguised… They are hiding behind ANGER, JEALOUSY & FEAR. They are hiding behind SILLINESS, INSECURITY & EXCUSES. Today I must tell you where to find them…
    Look in the mirror you'll find them…
You see?!?... You are Superman! You are Wonder Woman! You can save yourself…You have the tools…You have the Power…The only thing you don't have is the right attitude…Ask yourself, do you have the right attitude?

Change your attitude and your Life will begin to change!!!

Hey Super Man… The "S" on your chest is not a "S" at all. It's a forward "C" on top of a backwards "C". The forward "C" represents the change in you that's needed. It also suggests that you are going forward, seeing forward and thinking forward with your life. Life is tough!!!... You must become tougher…

The backwards "C" represents the YOU that you're leaving behind… No longer will you go backwards with your decisions, no longer backwards in your attitude, no longer backwards in your choices…Time has come for you to change… Start now, quit looking backwards, quit looking for excuses and began to "C" you going forward, "C" yourself accomplishing and achieving GREATNESS in your life…Greatness in your near future…

"OVERCOME" Words for YOU

Hey Wonder Woman, the "W" does not symbolize a weak person...It stands for a WINNER... It stands for a future WOMEN of Power...A WOMEN of GRACE...Inside the "W" there will be peaks and valleys...You must survive the dark valleys to enjoy the Peaks...Someday you will flip the "W" over and create an "M"...That "M" will mean that you have MASTERED your destiny! You can be a winner in life...and you can master your life...

Hey Super Man, Hey Wonder Women, don't be next to fall victim to the killer of dreams by smoking, snorting, doing drugs or by stealing. You're killing your dreams by arguing and fighting, and wasting your time tagging or writing fake names on broken fences or empty walls, hoping to hide your fake, broken and empty life. These are dream killers trapping you in a life unfit for your talents.

Be the first in your family to graduate from high school or college...
Be the first to buy Mom a new Car...
Be the first to purchase school clothing or supplies for a Younger sibling (brother or sister)...
Be the first in your Family to blaze a trail or pathway for others to follow.

Life is tough. You must be TOUGHER. No Excuses Produces...Remember

"A brilliant idea or talent trapped in a lazy mind is a death sentence for your GREATNESS"

Hey Superman...
Hey Wonder Women...
You can MASTER
your own life!

"OVERCOME" Words for YOU

Get Ready...
The Fix is Coming...

If you can't FIX your ANGER ...
If your Mother can't FIX your ATTITUDE...
If your Grandmother can't FIX your SPIRIT...
You better get ready because "Rock Bottom" is about to FIX all three, plus humble you...

Coach Etheridge

"You must learn to Let things Go!

Today we will discuss the importance of letting things go. Sometimes we waste precious energy and time holding on to nonsense.

As I see people interacting with one another everyday arguing, fussing, cussing, fighting, being disrespectful over things that don't really matter or have any significance. Young folks caring more about gang colors and tag names, many of them are taking more pride in tag names that they paint everywhere, on walls, street signs than their birth name. Birth names are being valued less than street names. Young people seem to be living for conflicts, even fighting across the internet on Facebook, Instagram, Kik, or Snapchat.

"You must learn to let things go"

We sometime get angry when our name was not called to recognize our contribution to the team's success. We carry grudges because of disagreements for days instead of moving on. We fight for parking spaces or get angry because of being cut off while driving. At times our immaturity forces everyone to get upset over the most insignificant reasons such as; he looked at me wrong, she said something under her breath, she rolled her eyes, or what are they laughing at…I saw a lady at the grocery store get upset in the

15 items and under line, because the customer ahead of her had eighteen items. "Come on Man!!!
"You must learn to let things go"

Reality shows are robbing our youth from the reality of respect to perpetuate shock ratings. Boys that have ignorant conflict with girls become Men that beat and disrespect women or their wives. Girls and boys continue lashing out because of maybe a missing man or missing women in their life. Children running the streets because their mother has given up and don't care. Parents too tired to demand the respect they deserve, so they speak disrespectfully themselves. Girls continue to speak cruel words to destroy and inflict the ultimate pain.

"You must learn to let things go"

Letting things go is a learned behavior that you must begin to practice. You must separate your treasures of life from the trash in life. You must practice this in order to reach your potential. If you have hopes of becoming a good father, good husband, good mother, or good wife… Recognize that you're in training right now…Start changing, start training today…If you want to have a great job, or want have a great career, or simply a better life than what you have now, then recognize you are in training right now…***This is what we definitely know…***
We know what- a disruptive boy looks like on the path of being a poor father…9-1-1 will be called your private line…. 9-1-1 is not a Joke!!!

-**We know what** a confused girl looks like; a victim of domestic violence and locked in a future of abuse and irresponsibility.
-**We know what** angry kid looks like on a fast track to the grave.
-**We know what** a beaten down, no hope having teenage girl looks like, that's going to become a beaten down, no hope having mother.
-**We know what** a frustrated, humiliated, uneducated drop-out with no job looks like.
-**We recognize** depression in the eye of a mother, or the frustration of a father whose boy has been lost to the streets, gangs, or drugs.
-**We know what** a fatherless pregnant teenager (who happens to be a child herself) looks like, that chooses to bring a fatherless baby into this world so she can have someone to love. And unfortunately **we also know what a child in a casket looks like…**

You now have a chance to start changing. It's not too late for you. It's not smart to continue a tragic path and let a "tragic moments change you forever…or you can take control of your DESTINY.

As we look into the eyes of fatherless girls, or girls acting out because the need for attention, we wonder why and when did stupidity become more important or logical than common sense…SUCCESS…

"You've got to learn to let things go"!!!
Ignore conversations or comments that get in the way of your fresh start. Prioritize what's important

to you. Memorize your path to success and start crawling, start walking, start running to get there.

"Start changing today... If you have hopes of becoming a good father, good husband, good mother, or good wife... Recognize that you're in training right now...Start changing today, start training today. You are in training right now"

You may be a struggling boy, girl, teen, parent, husband, wife, college student, in any profession. Your struggles may not be about you at all, it may be your situation, your job, your friends, your school, your home, and even your church. Don't be afraid to "GET OUT or GET AWAY or GET FIXED, or GET RIGHT…

No one is immune from "The Struggle".

Sometimes a changed in the situation or even your mindset will result in the change you need. There will come a point in your life where "The Struggle" will slap you in the face. **Fight back! Push back! Don't ever give up!**

<u>Cry, Survive, Revive, and then THRIVE you must!!!</u>

> "Sometimes you need to go backwards with a student in order to go forward with the student"
>
> You must go backwards to discover the student to make it possible to move forward to motivate the student"

Handling the angry parent...
Refer to the 3-H's

1. **HEAR**...hear them out...allow room to vent...listen to the concern...
2. **HELP**...help them... search to solve...find a workable balance... explain solution... don't take away dignity, leave it...
3. **HELLO**...follow-up with a phone call. Communication will win the parent, and then you will win the student.

The Beauty of a Rose

The beauty of a ROSE is its aroma, its strength, its courage, its ability to stand alone at the top of its stem, its ability to survive the weather...raging storms and searing heat. ..

A ROSE has the ability to project smiles just by being, a ROSE has the ability to bring light to darken hearts just by being, and a ROSE has the ability to lift burdens off its petals just by being... The petals of a ROSE provide protection, joy, and beauty to a sometimes lonely, difficult world...

Women are the ROSE'S... and their children are their petals of her joy, their petals of her beauty, their petals of protection, and their petals to escape the loneliness or the struggle of a frowning world... The petals protect the heart of the ROSE...

The petals of a ROSE are significant and we must ACCEPT its petals, bruise or slightly bruised...We must accept the children...for the children are vital to a mother's happiness. Women with children are beautiful.

The ROSE stands strong...She endures the weather. She stands alone at the top, respected and surrounded by beautiful petals...

Our ROSES come in all shapes, colors, and sizes... Never laugh our dishonor a ROSE because you don't understand her journey. Never frown at a ROSE because of its many petals, or bruised petals...

ROSES bring happiness, strength, and provide light to places you could never attend or go... Oh God, thank you for the beautiful ROSES...We can't survive without them... Respect all women...for they are ROSES...They may not be your ROSE but always remember they belong to someone and more importantly God's hand created them...

Hey Guys, quit missing out. Roses with pedals are beautiful and can be vessels to your happiness or completeness. Those that speak negatively of ROSES, themselves are the haters of beauty, haters of wisdom, hater of children... and haters of God... Don't be foolish...

If someone is laughing or disrespecting ROSES,
"Check them until they RESPECT them"...
I was raised by a ROSE and I live with a ROSE...
Change is coming. You better get ready...

"OVERCOME" Words for YOU

"Put the Gun Down"

*My mind racing, chasing, flying and trying to understand
The message escaping my mind is why the senseless killing of the Black Man*

*I've got to do something, what can I do?
Enraged with so much anger, I'm destined to become a victim too*

*Then my family will become double-victims of those that KILL
Another angry Father loss because of his protest and Goodwill*

*Everyone should be enraged by the "Bullets to the Back"
Outrage from UNIVERSAL colors, Red, White, Brown, not only Black*

*Universal Rage for the Truth and to Discover
Are we bringing harm to America for not protecting its Brothers?*

*Fines and Jail time to protect our animals, even hungry Cats
Homeless Dogs, certain Frogs, and even tested lab Rats*

Outrageous rage for outrageous rage can often be heard
Protection of bald eagles, certain flowers, and even the Birds

NRA protection for "Suited Thugs" to carry loaded Guns
Stupidly believing "God, Guns, and Country is America's goal #1

Their God has to be false; their Guns should be lost, because America continues to pay the cost
Because ignorance is shooting us down, to prove superiority or who's the boss

These Thugs are no different than the Thugs of ISIS
They are ruthless, toothless and their personal hate creates a Universal CRISIS

Their arrogance and boldness,
Continues to prove they're soulless
As they commit MURDER
Their eyes only display coldness

This is depressing, do we need to quit watching the News
Hell No! The News must change for something better "We can use"

*The real cowards are passing the Laws
Passing legislation to keep "The Black Clause"*

*Look at the Senate and House, notice how the Congress continue to Act
This is not made up, it's a TRAGIC FACT*

Quit fixing MORE with LESS...LESS with STRESS... STRESS with MESS... Quit fixing MESS with the ultimate TEST...

"The worst feeling I ever had in my life was to see my Mother Cry"

"I would rather die than see my Mother cry…"

"OVERCOME" Words for YOU

Greatness... flawed Greatness...

-Dedicated to Grandmother's-

As I think of the greatest people that I've ever met, I must admit among their greatness, imperfection was often lying dormant in their beings.

"Greatness has nothing to do with living a perfect life, but a life of impact has everything to do with Greatness"

The most impactful person I ever met was my grandmother... Don't get me wrong, my mother has done the most for me but may Grandmother has had the biggest impact on me and so many others.

Grandmothers are so special because the grandchild sees the Granny fix problems that the Mother cannot solve. The grandchild witnesses as the grandmother teaches, scolds, and nurtures their mother. Mother's do their best keep it together, but when mother's become overwhelmed. Grandmothers step in and wrap their arms around the troubles of life. Grandmothers will keep your household together and the household of the others. Grandmothers step in with their medicine chest of miracles. She begins to hug your troubles away, run your fears off, and lift you to a better place...

"A grandmother's bosom and apron, is a medicine chest that's filled with tenderness, band aids, forgiveness, ice packs, patience, aspirin, advice, needle and thread, compassion, tape, discipline, and wisdom"

If not for Grandmothers where would families end up? I lost my Grandmother over twenty years ago yet her impact still is prevalent daily in our family and the families of others... In her absence she continues to urges our family to hold on and fix problems every day. That is Greatness!!! That's the impact of Greatness...

You see we are not perfect...Everyone has imperfection lying around hoping to surface at the most inopportune moment. You must understand the life of MAN is perfectly imperfect.

So don't be shocked or surprised. Imperfection allows us to experience the greatest tools God has given us. The tools of FORGIVENESS, the tools of COMPASSION, and his tool of MERCY...

As we grow we began to gain experience and overcome our imperfections. We champion in hope, we champion in sacrifice and discipline at the same time. Strength is built thru weaknesses for others to witness, recognize and acknowledge.

As we get a grip on our imperfection, we began to enjoy the sunrise of God's forgiveness, his compassion, and his mercy. A beautiful painting inside an old worn wooded frame, dotted with the markings of life, is still a beautiful painting. The marking of its frame improves the beauty of the painting. The grandmother (the frame) has life's worn markings, yet she remains the pillar of greatness...

The imperfections of life create the peaks and valleys of pain, achievement, and happiness. The journeys that we overcome, allows us to appreciate the grandmothers courageous past, which created her courageous wisdom...

There are some great women out there, Mothers, and Grandmothers that have overcome tragedies in their life... Overcome a life of abuse, the loss of a child, and has overcome being minimized as a person for others to be maximized...

I toast you today with the wine glass full of the living water that drove your thirst to survive, accept, and thrive... Thank you God for their Greatness....flawed Greatness...

STANDARDS

If you attempt to teach troubled students to rise to YOUR STANDards, many times the troubled student will rebel...

But if you teach the troubled student to rise to the standards that their mother PLANTED in them at Birth...Or to the standards their grandmother envisioned, THEY WILL LISTEN

Coach Etheridge

Know Your Purpose

Today, in this section I will share a conversation with you about knowing your purpose. Prepare for the storm while serving that in which you are.

You can't allow people to get in the way of your purpose. Others may have their own idea on who you should be for them or what you should become. There is a huge difference in someone giving you a vision and someone impairing your vision to success.

Visions are powerful for success...
But can also be obstacles to success...

Also we must not get in our own way...I've witnessed a normal military family become a Cowboy family because of one Man's vision. This man provided the vision for a family and now that family has three generations of Cowboys. If a vision, belief, and God's approval is all you need, well now is time for you to hit the road. God's purpose for you may be different. God has given us talents to serve humanity. **You must walk in the strength in which you are.** Sometimes you may not understand your path. Your faith must sustain you in moments of doubt...

I'm reminded of the path of Moses. As Moses and his people wondered for forty years in the desert basically walking in circles with faith, so may be your path at this moment. Your path may seem like a tireless circle right now, but with God on your side you must be willing to wander tirelessly, you must be willing to wander wearily, and you must be willing to wander aimlessly. Your FAITH is going to be tested…

If it's God's purposes that you are serving then do your wandering with fierce dedication.

You must lock your faith. You must lock your commitment. You must lock your passion.

You must set the alarm to alert you of the thieves of temptation. The bad weather or hurricane siren to warn you of danger lurking… Guess what? Noah didn't have a hurricane siren to warn of bad weather. He stood on his faith and God's word (alone) to warn others. Someone may try to steal your passion, steal your certainty, and steal your focus. They are trying to kidnap your commitment to God. Today, we must take a stand against anything that is against us and anyone that is against our purpose. We must be able to ignore family, friends, co-workers, that do not understand our path. Your talents must be used to please God and fulfill his purpose.

"If you fulfill Man's purpose, all he can give you is a smile and a handshake…But if you fulfill GOD'S purpose, you receive your SALVATION"

Sometimes we don't know where our NEXT is coming from…our next meal, drink, or blessing. We may not know where our next check, next job, or even our next

"We don't even worry about the next when we are in our purpose. We only concern ourselves with being the next for someone else"

friend will come from, but if we are serving our purpose God will bring us a next…

Have you been a next for someone lately, have you been the next friend in need. Everyone sympathizes and wants to feed the hungry child, but what about the hungry child of God. That hungry child may be 40,50, or 60 years old.

God's children are ageless and come in all shapes sizes and colors. Even the purpose riders, (those riding their purpose) need help. "Purpose Riders" are still dependent on blessing from others to stay on God's path for their own ride of life. At times you may be low on gas, low on energy, or low on knowledge. It's time to ride it out on faith… Faith… Faith… Sometimes the spouse may not understand their mate's purpose. We hope that's not the case but it may be so. Even your children may not agree or understand your purpose because they may be too young to comprehend.

Your "What's my purpose" conversation should be a private meeting between you and God. Your conversation with God can remain between you and him. When you fast (from food) you shouldn't shout to the world your sacrifice "I'm not eating for thirty days"…Whisper it to God in the closet and ask for strength to endure. We should counsel with the Lord in the closet about our plans. "Huddle up and call the play"… The devil is trying to see your plans"… Something's are for personal, private counsel with the Lord.

I saw a guy wear a red suit to church one Sunday, he was definitely seen and heard on that Sunday. His presence commanded attention. The attention getting bright and brilliant clothing could not be over looked. This reminds me that sometimes women dress suggestively, or skimpily to attract sexual attention rather than respectful attention. The young man at church with the bright colored suit was demanding attention, (or all his other suits may have been dirty). Same with the sexy dressed teen heading to the Mall or to the Movies wearing to too little shorts or the revealing blouse. Some will gossip and share opinions good or bad regarding inappropriate dress. But when the young man wore his dark suit to church to serve others, his service was the focus, not the color of his suit. Also when girls, ladies, women dress in respect for their bodies, they attract respect. It's better to attract respectful people in your life.

Most men want to marry a beautiful princess. Most women dream of marrying caring selfless men.

God wants humbled servants that are respected due to their service to humanity rather than Man's materialistic distractions.

When we begin to focus on the needs of us, them, they, and the needs theirs…

…THEN GOD WILL THEN SERVE YOU…

Win The Day!

A message to share today is to remind you that we are happy you've grown into your presence. But we can hardly wait to see growth in your purpose. Each day spend more time appreciating the now, the today. Spend a little less time (10%) dreaming of tomorrow and focus on doing (90%) today.

Active day's make attractive tomorrows...
Inactive day's make reactive tomorrows...
Be active, alert, and eager each day....

Just as the birds live for today without worry, so should we. Birds do not worry or hunger for tomorrow, They fly around (working), save and prepare for the future and so should we. Birds seem to understand that there is an endless supply of food for them, as long as they continue to fly and move around (work). The fields, the grass, the trees, fruit, provide an abundant amount of food for all flying fowl. God has even provided the birds with the ability to migrate great distances to eat. Birds can even take advantage of the waste of man…the French fries thrown from the car window…the unfinished apple core, or the uneaten bread from a sandwich.

Matthew Chapter 6 30-33 says
30—Wherefore, if God so clothe the grass of the field, which the day is and tomorrow is cast into the oven, shall he not much more clothe you, O ye of little faith?
31)—Therefore take no thought, saying. What shall we eat? Or, what shall we drink? Or Wherewithal shall we be clothed?
32)—for your heavenly Father knoweth it that ye need all of these things.
33)—But seek ye first the kingdom of God and His righteousness and all these things shall be added unto you.

So, we should follow the example. God has provided us with endless supply to meet our needs, and to address our concerns. Through us he has provided rest for the weary, through us he has provided food for the hungry; through us he will provide peace for those seeking war.

Oh I remember the first prayer my Mom taught me…

"God is great; God is good, let us thank him for our food. Amen"

As we walk and discover our path, our purpose, we must be unyielding in our judgment of sharp objects, keenly aware of dangerous setbacks in the road.

We must anticipate sharp objects or poor decisions will flatten our tires or detour our futures. We need flat proof Michelin tires to avoid those dangers, and we need more importantly a God proof plan to fulfill HIS purpose for us.

"His mission is our position"

Matthew Chpt.4 -16 reads; The People which sat in Darkness saw great Light. And to them which sat in the region and shadow of death Light is sprung...

Get up; Step up; Start up; protect his mission with your key in the ignition. You are the key, recognize your purpose, and recognize your talent to fulfill your purpose...

"Get out of you and get into him. Get into him and move away from them".

Go to your closet and devise the plan, the purpose for your life. Don't be afraid... Ask God for patience and understanding, knowledge, and gas money for the trip of your life...

> **Being A Father is Tough,**
>
> **But Being Fatherless**
>
> **Is Pure Hell!!!**
>
> **I like it Tough...**

What's up Old Man?

Today, I'm going to talk / share with you a conversation I had with a student that change his life, change his direction. The words were simply too overwhelming and powerful. Sometimes tough words or tough love equals save words or save love
(How old are you?)

What's up old Man? I would ask this particular student everyday as I took roll before I would start teaching the assignment of the day.

ROLL CALL...I would call each student's name for roll call and they in turn would answer "here or present" in their own unique way. Roderick, *here Coach E...* Anthony, *I'm present Coach...*Broshawn, *back here Coach...*Fonda, *you know it Coach...*Lisa, *best student is here Coach...* Tony, *right here Sir...*Raymond, *waiting on you Sir...* Ricky, *hey coach...*Sherry, *right here always...*

Then I would get to the young man sitting on the back row. He would always sit quietly, head slumping down, either he was tired from the previous night activities or just disinterested in the assignment that was to follow roll call. Then, I would call his name... **OLD MAN**"; he would give a slight head nod to at least acknowledge he was present without using the little energy he had left. He was street tired...no rest...

The other student would kind of look at me strangely, but dared not ask why I called him "old Man". So I continued, Sheila, *I'm here sir...* Jackie...*"me and my brand new shoes are her today Coach"*...Thanks I would reply... Then I would begin teaching the days assignment...I would always call all the other students by their official (first) birth name.
But as I got to this one particular student name, I would always break the normal routine and refer to him as **"OLD MAN"**. The other students assumed it was his nickname because he was always tired.

Finally after about a month or so into the school year, the other student finally gained enough nerve to ask the tired boy. Why does he call you "old Man"? The tired boy then sort of smiled and said "I don't know? I think he really thinks I'm cool or something...Ask him why! Ask him why as they continued to encourage the tired boy to ask me…No, you ask him if you want to know so bad…Oh, you must be scared to ask Coach why…The tired boy didn't want anyone to feel he was afraid of anything. So he accepted the challenge. *Coach, why do you call me "old Man", that's not my name. You're the only teacher in this school call me that… Why?*

Finally, I had waited on this question since the beginning of the school year. The class was quiet, you could hear a pin drop…Every classroom eye was on me…

I began to tell a story about the journey of an old man. I saw an old man long ago crossing the street near a nursing home. As I stopped to help him, he explained that he had been very sick. He stated that he was living with strangers in the nursing home. He was old, gray, weak and unstable. "My life has had many ups and downs, but most of my downs were due to my poor decisions. He continued to say

"I'm eighty-five (85) years old and I don't have very many years left. Son, I'm kind of tired, he stated. Maybe one or two years left to live at the most".

Well, I call this student (pointing to him) sitting in this desk, "old Man" because he doesn't have much

time left...one or two years at the most. You are also like the old Man crossing the street. You are close to the end (as I pointed toward him again). **His eyes opened wide "like a deer in headlights".** I caught him completely off guard as I went into a verbal tirade into his troubled world. You're in the streets, making the fast money. Dealing with the dirty night life... Son, you're playing Russian roulette with a six-shootout, but with five bullets in the chamber. Only one chamber is empty.

You're about to die...You may not be here tomorrow...You want to "Get Rich or Die trying in reality You want to "Die early and get Rich" lying... You, young man, have become deaf. You have become mute...you can't talk or communicate with your family...Just like the real Old Man existing in the nursing home.

Strangers are watching you Die...just as the old Man's environment in the nursing home...Stranger's don't care about your dangers...It's easier to look the other way.

Your family tried to talk and care.
But you only yelled and continue to stare.

Get out! Your mom screamed at you.
"I brought you into this world; I will take you out,
Get out Now!"

Then you screamed back "I'm Out Mama!
Then drugs, crime, and the streets then took you IN!

Just look at yourself "OLD MAN"!!!
Your beautiful brown eyes are now dirty brown...
Your beautiful smooth lips are now chocolate chips...
Once you had beautiful skin, but now, it's like a broken street light, scary, blotchy, and darkened like on a streets dead end.

"Hey old Man, WAKE UP!
You can become young again.
Change your ways...Fix your pain!
Fix your anger! Fix your damn pants!"
I hear universal remote controls will give power to almost every TV, except for the "old ones". Be a universal remote for who you want to become. Turn off the power of what you use to be and turn on the power to become someone better. He then put his head down for the rest of the period...He dared not challenge my tirade because he knew that I cared and was his favorite teacher...

That boy missed a few days of class after that day. He later explained that he missed those days of school to fix his relationship with his mother and family. Upon his return, he was a different person. He dressed differently, he walked differently, and he sat at his desk differently. As I began to check roll soon I came to his name, I said.
"What's up Donell? Looking good young Fella
He smiled…the class gave him a standing ovation with applause included. He hugged and thanked the roll call leader…
I never called him "Old Man" again, He lives today…

"Sometimes your greatest achievements in life are the one's unknown to you"

Coach Etheridge

"OVERCOME

"When someone has been good to you or has done good by you for years...

Don't allow a bad decision to fill your heart with regret for the GOOD years..."

I thank you for the good years...

If you decide to go...you must also let the anger and the disappointment go...

Stay in the positive to recognize the next POSTITIVE....

"Sometimes things happen in LIFE that are never repaired...

But we must pick up the pieces and create a better life from the usable pieces remaining"

Coach Etheridge

"OVERCOME" Words for YOU

They Will Never Forget

The troubled person will never forget what you done for them. He will remember the wrinkled $20 you gave him, when he was down and out for the count...He will never forget that day you ask him to look into your eyes and be a Man of principle instead of a boy who thought he was invincible...

She will remember the encouragement that you gave her with your smile that saved her...Saved her from her secret to end it all... The hug you gave that day hugged away the unknown tragedy of suicide...The guidance and groceries you delivered that day fed more than her stomach, it fed her SOUL...You saved a family that day from a tragic moment.

The day HE just needed a Daddy figure to make sense of the world...and you said the magic words "I'm not your Daddy but I'm gonna be a Daddy for you"... Now listen Son go to school, graduate, I got you're back...Let go of the anger, it will only lead to danger... He will always remember your looks of disappointment then the quick refocus of your face to say "that's alright, I did that too when I was your age"...

She will remember the words written on the wrinkled napkin from her mother or grandmother left on the counter...telling her to hold on God's coming... and it's $20 in the cup behind the coffee in the back of the cabinet...

He will remember the Man that treated him as if he was his own son... He will never forget the Man that grabbed him around his neck and said "Listen to me, you're better than that"...

She will remember the teacher that gave her the secret advice that saved her life... She was abandoned and pregnant...but she will always remember the advice of that teacher...so the young lady called her after all those years and she (the teacher) stepped into the moment again with her to save the day...because mistakes are a part of life...

"You can never hold your head down or let go of the rope. Someone held on because of you, now you must hold on because of them"...

"Sometimes things happen in LIFE that are never repaired, but we must pick up the pieces and create a better life from the usable pieces remaining"
Coach Etheridge

The German Chocolate Cake

The Baking of a Cake

My Aunt baked the best German Chocolate cakes ever. Her system of baking the perfect cake is well documented in my family. She would always say

"Baby, you must have the basic ingredients and a whole lot of patience."

Same with our lives, with some basic ingredients and patience we too can master our own destiny.

When baking a cake we must mix the ingredients thoroughly and follow the already proven process or the results will be different. The ingredients to a great tasting cake are always the same. A great cake should include flour, oil, sugar, milk, eggs, baking powder, and butter; these items are mandatory and universal for success. Without one of these ingredients, the cake will not turn out as intended.

What are the ingredients for a great Man or Women? What are the "must haves" to insure your success or that you will turn out as good as your favorite cake? As you go through the process of collecting, and mixing the ingredients, the timing and preparation will also determine the success of the cake. As you go through the process in life, the timing and preparation will also determine the success of your life. You must receive all the necessities to turn out right. You will need a good collection of family memories, mixed with a cup of your Mom's or Dad's personal experiences, and then add 2 tablespoons of extra strength wisdom from Grandma. Just as a good cake needs a couple of broken eggs, your life will need a couple of breaks also. Some people call fortunate breaks luck. Some people call fortunate breaks BLESSINGS. Your life must also follow a logical sequence. The timing and preparation in your life will also determine the success of your journey. With the right ingredients, the right patience, and the right timing, your blessing will flow abundantly.

Many of life's rewards occur during the journey, not at the end of it...

A mother's fondest memories of her adult child often reflect back to a time during the early years of life. Parents remember and enjoyed nurturing and teaching the child to take his or her first step. They will remember the first time the baby talked or mumbled Mama. Parents, especially Fathers remember teaching you to ride your first bike, or the first time he taught (forced) you to cut the grass, or clean the kitchen before your Mom got home from work. As a kid I remember my Mom teaching me to wash the dishes while my brother had to wash the pots. We would rotate every week... I still wash dishes today, without a complaint because it was instilled in me as a child. I'm sure my wife is happy my Mom taught me that. That's my part, that' my contribution, that's my responsibility.

Good parents will strive to teach their children basic values of life from the beginning to the end. Important values such as "it is better to give than receive" or many other concepts of love, such as Generosity-the gift of giving…or Compassion- the gift of caring. It's tough to learn those values after you leave the nest. In many cases that's too late. Your destination to greatness lies along the trails of the journey. Not after you get there…It occurs on the way. High school diploma requires twelve years of learning, not just on graduation day. The learning occurs before graduation day… The ingredients for a good cake must be mixed, stirred, and whipped before the cake is baked, so that the cake will taste good.

"Too many youngsters rush to tragedies, rather than pace their life with strategies"

To those of you that didn't make it to Graduation Day stop for a moment. Think back to those days and ask yourself why? What happened? At what point did you stop listening? At what point did you become deaf to the voices of concern. At what point did you began to think that you knew more than your parents… At what point did you simply become partners with the streets, drugs, sex, and life in the fast lane.

"Your life must include the proper ingredients for success. Too many young lives rush to tragedies, instead of pacing their life's moments with strategies."

A life without the proper patience or timing to nurture success will seem like a bad tasting cake.

<u>When you are a teen, don't rush to adult activities.</u>

Your life must be mix properly, or whip properly, or matured to your designed age (temperature). When you are a teenager, participate in activities that safe for teenagers. Have good safe fun. As an Adult you must let go of the childish behavior. The streets or street life will not gently stir you to perfection like your families loving hands. The streets of hard knocks will knock the hell out of you. It sure will hack away your spirit, your motivation and your common sense. The streets have turned good youngster into monsters that turned against their own families. **When did you become deaf to common sense?**

As a young child trying to bake my first cake, I have vivid memories of a smoke filled house. I didn't mix nor bake at the right temperature. The house was soon full of smoke and other odors…My eyes became irritated, my nose began to sneeze…I began to panic and my Mothers attitude was thunderous, quick, fast, and in a hurry…because something is being ruined… Smokey curtains, burnt pots, foul odors throughout the house are enough to run any mother crazy. If a Mother see's her child taking short cuts, she will get angry as if someone was ruining her good pots or smoking up and ruining her curtains.

Why abandon the follow the all-ready proven process…Stick to the keys so the cake will taste and smell good…As you grow ***you must allow*** *your (life) ingredients to be properly mixed.* ***You must allow*** *yourself to be thoroughly stirred.* ***You must allow*** *yourself to be whipped into shaped so that you can reach your potential.* ***Don't rush*** *to grown up activities. Neither your body nor your mind will be able to handle it.* ***Don't skip stages,*** *live the important moments, don't leave them.*

Value the meaningful relationships, don't ruin them. Allow yourself to feel complete. Allow achievement

to complete you, to make you excited and full of life. You must turn out to be someone your Mom, Dad, brother, sister, or Grandparents can be proud of. Just as the cake must turn out good, so should your life, for all to enjoy. Too many caring people have sacrificed for you to not have a life of achievement.
You must be tasty, moist, sweet, and soft, rough and thick. The cakes edgy icing will hold it together. Your family (the icing) is protection for (your) or the cakes perfection. A good cake must be;
*Tasty-**I mean you must be nice and polite...***
*Moist-**I'm saying you must be tender to the touch...***
*Sweet-**You must respect your elders, honor others.***
*Soft-**You must have a forgiving heart...have compassion for others...***
*Rough, thick, and edgy-**I'm suggesting that you be strong, stubborn, protective, focused, and resistant of stupidity and underachievement. You must "Get it together and keep it together"***
The spoon that stirs the cake is the loving arm of your mother hugging you, stroking you, gently guiding. The cake pan is the protection you needed from the outside world until you were able to protect yourself. Your parents, grandparents or someone has shared with you the keys of life.

"Don't ever give away what was given to you. Only share what was given to you. If you give it away, it's no longer within you. If you share it with someone, it's always a part of you and the person you shared it with. Remember; you don't have to be empty for someone else to be full. A caring person's sharing transcends generations to come."

RESPONSIBILY

The measure of a Man or Husband is not in his physical strength.

Simply look at his words and Deeds, and then notice the emotional weight lifted off his wife and children"

"Sometimes the strongest Men can only bench press a few pounds"

Guys make sure you're working out every day in the GYM of RESPONSIBILITY

Take care of your CHILDREN...

Coach Etheridge

"OVERCOME" Words for YOU

I Don't Know...
But I Do Know...

I don't know what it feels like to lose a Son
The Pain unbearable I know,
I've been a witness to more than one

Why the Violence,
Why death for what this unarmed youngster did?
Dead on the scene or dead on arrival,
He was so young, what a poor Kid

You had no right;
You had no right to take him from this Earth
He was a child Man!
His Mom sacrificed and gave Birth

The Time will come for you to die
Surprise! Bang or a Boom, no one will cry

The food is salty; the water has a bitter taste!
We are dying every day
Someone's trying to End my Race

The anger you provoke, to continue your waste
Step Back! We are "The Chosen Ones"
The descendants of Jake

Hallelujah, the time is here
My time has finally come
Home with my Savior

My path sacrificed before I was born
To my silencer
I live forever, never to leave your sight
As you lay,
I ride your sleep waves to continue the Fight

The scribbles darting and flying behind the closed
lids is not a kite
It's me flying high to wake you
To keep you up at Night

Your hunting of me yesterday
Will be my haunting of you forever
I'm at Peace with my God; you're at War…
…I'm better

I say stand strong, and remember my smile
To those I left behind
Victory is mine! Victory is mine! Victory is mine!

I'm not hungry but full, without strife or anger
At peace resting with Jesus, no longer in danger

I'm not thirsty but overflowing with abundant
glory, I say again without strife
He was crucified to save me, he paid for my Life

His message,
"Forgive them for they not know what they do"
Jesus did this for me;
"So I must do this for the silencer too"

I forgive my enemies that paved the way
Forever with my Savior, I achieve my Glory today.

"OVERCOME" Words for YOU

SeaSON'S Greeting

Baseball season is here.
Peanuts, popcorn and the crack of the bats
Reminds us of the guys wearing the baseball caps

Football season is here. Touchdown!
They continue to cheer!
With huge, spirited crowds that love their beer.

Deer Season is here,
Deer's running and jumping here and there.
Guns carried by hunters, aiming for food to share.

Black Season is here, what's Black season?
The season where it's okay to open fire
On a black man anytime, for any reason

Hands up! Where's your ID!
"Man, let me get my phone."
POW! POW! Another one gone,
A black man wasted on his way home.

Lining them up like carnival game,
Then shooting them down this is insane.

Mothers crying for an insane reason,
Sons are dying; due to a year-round killing season.

JANUARY, FEBRUARY, the months don't matter.
It's time to MARCH; angry Fathers are ready to splatter.
News cameras filming heart-broken death cries,
A mother's death cry should be for private eyes

Good cops continue to protect and serve
While suited thugs try to spark a nerve

Cops and Robbers their game the same
But suited thugs continue to blame the ones they slain

"The No Retreat Police" that carry guns,
Too bigoted to retreat back,
But forward they happily come.

Gun laws silenced, guns off the shelf they fly
While murdering thugs
Keep telling the sinister protected lie.

Self-defense, Self-defense, They don't have to retreat!!!
They felt fear
Because they saw black hands,
Or a hoodie, or heard the radio's bumping beat

It's me that should fear, I'm the threatened one,
They took a NRA (SELF) black defense class to kill and carry a gun

Following us around with membership card, and loaded gun,
Our only defense, a camera phone and witnesses of more than one…

Suited Thugs, shoot first, and then choke later
Blacks die first, and then sue later
Come on Man, this couldn't be your stand
God made every man a divine plan

Secret grand juries for public crimes,
The secrets out,
Whispering grand juries never bring justice to mine.

"OVERCOME" Words for YOU

Good people standing in protest of these Cowards,
The cowards then protest our protest,
They consider my race is even less

Stop this Madness! Stop their Gladness!
If it was your son, you would recognize the sadness.

Thank you God for helping us this far,
But we must help ourselves to fight this war

Voting is not the answer, they've rigged the system.
Hearts-broken parents continue to be double victims.

Women have protected our sons for years.
We must take a stand;
Or die fighting to eliminate those fears.

No longer at war with ourselves, unite now you see.
Time has come to fight the real enemy.

Dream... Dream... Is the dream still alive?
For my son to have his dream I'm willing to die

These are not the words of a famous rap star,
But the words of common educated man
That's been pushed too far!

Fight Hate!!! I'm ready to Die!!!

Season's Greetings

God Has Your Back

"God has your BACK, so use what he has given you to fix what's in FRONT"
-Matthew Chapter 5 1-17-

I saw a TV interview the other day; a young man was being interviewed after winning a basketball game. The young man referenced God in his response to the reporter stating, "God was with me, He gave me the strength to endure some tough times in my life. As the young man continued to talk, I listened intently and began to notice that his comments were more about the performance of his team rather than his individual success. He was a proud witness of God's grace and humility. This is uncommon, and often unfounded in today's me 1st, me 2nd, and me 3rd world.

Does God care about the winners and losers of games or contests I began to ponder? I thought hopefully his plate is too full of prayers for salvation. I hope God is not so petty as to be concern with my marble game when I was about 10 years old. It was a competition, it was fun, but it was just a game. I was very good and won a lot of marbles from the neighborhood kids... It was innocent and we were just having fun, and I had practiced for hours on hours to become a good player.

"I used what God had given me and fixed what was in front"...A strong thumb, good eyes and a straight aim. I'm not sure if God cared about my marble game but I know that God does care about you. Have you ever met a person that you immediately feel and see God's presence in their eyes? You can tell the moment you met them that something is special about this person... These people are Difference Makers... They are servants of God. The Winners (God's Servants) understand / accept / and value God's presence and GOD'S plan... You can see the Light of Love and compassion in their eyes... You can hear it in their voice... You can feel it in their touch ...

Many times, the Lost (Troubled) don't understand God's plan or recognize his presence. Many times they don't believe or accept God's has a plan for them. Many times they discount God's blessing to others as pure luck, or the result of unfair entitlement. As you look into the eyes of the troubled, do you see their darkness? Do you recognize the troubled spirit? As you listen to their voice or and their story, you hear hopelessness, despair, and negativity. When you touch them you feel their loneliness. You feel their defeat, you feel the emptiness, you feel the confusion, and you feel the sorrow. But when they look into your eyes what do they see...Do they see the RESCUERS light in your eyes? Do they recognize the eyes of God's winner? What do they see in you?

Matthew Chpt 4-16 reads; The People which sat in Darkness saw great Light. And to them which sat in the region and shadow of death Light is sprung...

Your Eyes-Do your eyes provide them with the LIGHT to chase their DARKNESS away... Do your eyes illuminate a PATH to God's greatness? A path of amazing journeys, amazing accomplishments, and amazing people that was lost but once they found God, their blessing found them...

Your Voice- Does your voice provide 1) hope, 2) inspiration, and 3) admiration? Hope to not give up, Inspiration to change to do better, Admiration because of your bravery to tell it like it is, to say it like it is, to preach it like it is. Does you Touch inspire security, faithfulness, rejuvenation. Does your touch create regret for the poor decisions?

God's plan is better than that of any man. "God has got our back, so we must use what he's given us to fix what's in front".

What can we do? You sometimes may ask yourself. Because of the overwhelming odds of a cruel world despair is in every corner...God has given us unlimited weapons and unlimited ammunition to win... Difference Makers are well armed for victory. We have many weapons for victory, but today I will speak of five. Let's review the powerful (5) weapons of victory.

1- Our Eyes-let everyone see God's light in your eyes...
2- Our Voice-let everyone hear the greatness of god's plan...What he has done for you is not secret...

3- **Our Ears**-Listen to their story let them know they are not alone...Sometimes you just need to listen
4- **Our Touch**-feel their Pain...Hold their hands...allow them to feel God's presence
5- **God's Mercy**- the Power of Prayer is amazing to the soul...

We have many weapons to use to win the lost or at least get them on the right path. It only takes ONE of these weapons to change someone... Our odds are now overwhelming for a successful turnaround for the troubled, weary, and disconnected. **"God has your back, so use what he has given you to fix what's in front"** Despair and anguish look for dark corner to hide. Despair may be in every corner but God's Power and Grace and Victory is everywhere! Despair may be in every corner but the world is round, not square. You can't find corners in a circle...You can't hide...God see's you! We see you... You're corner of darkness is located in a Circle of Light... Unlock your mind...Open your eyes...Unplug your Ears... Put some lotion or moisturizer on your hands so you can feel God touching you thru his servants.

As a boy, I cut the yard once with an old vibrating lawn mower...My grandmother paid me with soda bottles that I had to sell back to the store. The next day I developed hardened callouses on my hands...my hands were rough and calloused... Everyone I shook hands with complained about the unpleasant touch of my rough hands...I could not feel the discomfort of others because of the roughness of my skin. I then pulled the dead skin off my palms to soften my touch.

As I shook hand or reached for items my hand were so tender and sensitive to the touch that I felt excruciating pain every time I touched someone or shook their hand. I don't know if they felt my pain but I sure did. Could that be you today? Do you feel your pain and no one else's? Jesus felt your pan as he hung on the Cross. Remove hardened callouses from your unfeeling hands. Remove hardened callouses from your unfeeling heart and become sensitive of others.

Feel their pain because JESUS removed callouses for YOU a long time ago...Today the Son of God, Jesus is reaching out to you... Can you feel him...Are you listening to Him...Ask him to help you...Ask him to forgive you...Figure out and accept his plan for you, not your plan for him...

HELLO--- God's servants (The winners)-This is what we face. The lost must find their path thru us. We, all of us at times feel over-whelmed with the evil of the world. Your eyes can provide the path out, the light to chase away the darkness, the compassioned eyes... Your touch should provide the touch of spiritual peace...the touch of calmness and rejuvenation... the touch of the Greatness from God...

Your Voice can provide a voice of reason, the sound of faithfulness, and the whisper of encouragement. Your Ears listening is simply the ink in the pen that marks the paper saying to that person **"You are somebody and you are not a Lie"**...Remember...

"God has your BACK, so use what he has given you to fix what's in FRONT"

What are you fighting for?

I will not fight a Lie…But I will fight for the truth that's inside of me…If you question me {or my integrity} with a lie or falsehood, I will smile, I may even frown a little, but I will walk away. I will not waste my time because I know who I am and that which is within me is mine to give. But if you question these things; my commitment to God, my commitment to family, my commitment to my future, or my commitment to be a good parent someday, then I will defend, you should be prepared for a fight to the end. I'm willing to die for my God, my family, and my future because my future equates to the future of my children and grandchildren. I will defend honor of truthfulness, I will defend honor of family values, and I will defend the hopes of the future.

"That is a combination of values that I must keep for me"

I see young people distracted much of the time with defending someone else's lie. If the truth is in you, then that is what is important. The things outside come from unknown places, those can prove to be a lie. Don't get distracted with outside obstacles / distractions. Let distractions stay in their place (outside) Fight for what's inside of you and if what's inside of you is not good…put some sugar in you to sweeten your tastes…oh I'm not talking about "sweet and low"…I'm talking about "Sweet and High"…the sweetener you need is waiting on you today…He will stir you, season you, complete you…

Sometimes the obstacles of others are in place to distract you from your own journey. Sometimes we get caught up in someone else's anger, hate, or unfairness that began with a lie; meanwhile our very own journey to truth or victory was avoided or delayed. A lie is can be so swift and so fast. The truth is slow and patient. <u>WE</u> can't chase a lie; it operates at times at the speed of sound. But the truth is present always if you're patient enough to recognize it.

Most Mothers teach and instilled HONOR,
If we surrender that then we are surrendering her presence.
Most Grandmothers teach and instilled RESPECT
If we surrender that then we are surrendering her presence.
Their sacrifice Man!!!
"LET'S FIGHT RIGHT NOW!"

If you were raised without a mother, father, grandmother, grandfather, and then you probably had some tough times in your life. I always believed

"Tough times make appreciative Minds".
"Unfortunate beds make brilliant Heads".

But because Jesus hung on Calvary's Cross, God even gives you the choice for eternal life. I hope that you are lucky enough to be saved as you read this. What choices are you making today in your life. What are you fighting for? Who are you fighting for? Are you spending too much time fighting a losing battle? Hello, I hope you are listening today…

I once read a quote from Joel Osteen, he said, "We need to be known for what we are FOR and not for what we are AGAINST". Many of our so called leaders are riding the bitterness lane of hate. They take a stand against this or against that. I'm standing up today to tell you I'm taking a stand too. I'm taking a stand for good fathers, (are you?) I'm for good mothers, (are you?) I'm for good husbands, (are you?) and I'm for good wives, (are you?) so when you come across a youngster needing direction…GUIDE THEM, give them a vision, and give them direction away from their present circumstances.

We are for high school and college graduates, (are you?)

We are for young people respecting old people (are you?) and we are for hearing young boys and girls laugh (are you).

We are for middle school students yelling to support their teams, instead of yelling to ridicule them…

We are for seeing prideful smiles on young faces without feeling suspicious…

We are for those of you willing to sacrifice.

We are for those of you willing to keep your grandmothers hope alive.

We are for those of you willing to send straight cash to your mother for the rest of her natural life because of what she did for you. We are for those of you refusing to allow where you come from, stop you from where you going or where you should be.

We are for our youngsters learning the true meaning of hard work…

We are for those of you willing to let go of who they use to be, to become someone else. This can be you… This will be you…This is you… We are waiting for this you to arrive…

I know what you stand for today because you've confessed it with you voice. What do you confess today with your heart? The change you have been waiting for is here! Change now…God wants you to change now…Hallelujah, if there is someone here today reading this passage or hearing this message. Don't think about it "Just Do It" like the Nike logo says…But today it's the Jesus logo speaking to you…. "Just Do It". Come on up now….Go find you a church and confess. I believe the Christ died on that Cross for me to be saved today. Lift your hands; raise your heart to the heavens today as he was raised to the Heavens on the Sunday after three days of lock down. Your three days are up! It's time for you to rise up and serve your purpose. Repeat I accept Jesus as my Lord and Savior. It is done… Now go! Go now to fulfill his purpose in your life.

Today is a celebration of life, today is a celebration of love, and today is a celebration of hope. Be careful today, I'm willing to die…Don't get in my way… Thru Jesus, he is the Light…Thru Jesus, he is the Love…Thru Jesus; he is the Hope… If you don't want it, get out the way! Don't get in the way of those that do want it or may need it…Those that need Jesus today…Oh we need a hero today.

Superman jumped tall buildings on a single bound, Batman, saved Gotham city from darkness. My Hero raised Lazarus from the dead; My Hero, Jesus then

"OVERCOME" Words for YOU

went on to save the World from darkness... Who's your hero? Jesus is his name, Jesus, there's something about the name of Jesus...Something about the name of Batman just don't sound right. Something about the name of Superman doesn't sound right either.

But something about the name of Jesus does something to your soul...

Like I stated at the beginning, I will say it again but I will include you this time. WE will not fight a lie. But WE will fight for the truth to the end...If you question OUR integrity with a lie or falsehood, WE will smile, WE will walk away, WE will not waste our time because WE know who WE are. But if you question OUR commitment to God, to family, to OUR future, or OUR ability to be good parents someday, then WE will defend... Be prepared for a fight to the end. If we are willing to live because of God's blessings then we must be willing to die to have them for eternity.

Today, I say to those of you involved in gangs, hood or color, I have a message for you. Don't be willing to die because of some gang or color unless the color is "Jesus gold". Don't die for some silly Hood (Eastside, Westside, Southside, North side)...unless that Hood is inside the pearly gates, don't die for a homeboy simply because you both grew up together in the struggle without a Daddy, unless that daddy was the greatest Father of All...Jesus is his name. Like Lionel Richie said "Father, help your children, so they may not fall by the SIDE of the road". Father God, I thank you today for this powerful message...

"Being raised in a single parent household has given me unlimited fuel for success"

"My Mother and Grandmother gave me an Alternative Fuel"

Feeling A Little Empty Today?

First I would like to take a moment to reflect on the lives of those lost. But before I do that I must tell you that **_"Tragic moments can be the birth of greatness"_**. More often than not leaders, the difference makers come from moments of tragedy that changed their lives.

I'm sure your lost love one was probably a tremendously good person to you. I too cry every day because of the loss of loved ones. The pain never goes away but we must learn to live with the loss. Every day we all are reminded in some small day dreaming moment to think of a lost love one.

I often see heartfelt messages of from mothers, brothers, sisters, children; friends about all missing lost love ones. You are simply trying to find something to hold on too. Understand that you will always have an empty space, empty plate, empty chair, empty cup, an emptiness that can never be filled because of your loss.

But you know what?
"Sometimes I rather live with that emptiness,
to remember their greatness,
than to be full and to forget the lost".

We will always love the lost missing one. We will always miss them. We must learn to cherish the emptiness of their loss. We should always remember their smile, so we will smile at others. We should always be good friends because they were good friends to us. We will soon begin to feel better knowing what they (lost love one) did for all of us…Maybe their purpose was served; now we must serve our purpose. May God bless you and keep you…So to you I say today…

"Be proud to be a little empty today…The lost has given us something to remember them for"

Additional words for those that lost Mothers, Dads, Sisters, Brothers, Uncles, Aunts, and Friends

"I smiled today because of their smile yesterday. I dreamed today because their dreams yesterday. I live in this difficult time right now because their smiles and dreams are with me forever"

"Graduation Day"

This is a conversation I have with students about Graduation Day. My goal is to provide them with a glorious vision of their future. But remind them that the journey is full of obstacles. Graduation Day is a day for family, friends, and a time to be very thankful for the unknown sacrifices of those that help you get to this great Day... Words to the student...

Someday you will hopefully walk across the stage on Graduation Day...On that day; your name will be called to signify the completion of your education. On Graduation Day...You will receive a diploma; but your parents and grandparents will be receiving much more. The answers too many of their prayer are being answered on that day. Your family will hope that you have received their wisdom, their kindness, their understanding, and their sense of pride in family.

Your parents will have hoped that you understand the value of love, compassion, and respect, but anticipating love, compassion, and respect in return. I can only imagine what your Mother went thru to get you here. She carried you for nine months of discomfort. The great sacrifice she made for you, wobbling down the hospital hall, enduring the pain of your birth that was to come. The joy of an adoptive parent has in receiving the blessing of a child to love. Their only request is for a beautiful healthy child. The responsibility of raising a child in today's world is very tough. Many people have worked hard to get you to this moment.

In a short time you will be walking across the stage on graduation day. That will be a great moment for you. The family will arrive in their best dressed clothing to witness your day. Your Mom or grandmother will cook a great meal or take the family out to celebrate your day. Your favorite uncle or cousin may slide up to you and issue a few extra dollar bills to increase your graduation pocket. Be thankful because there are some classmates that did not make it to this day. The poor decisions and mistakes that they rush into came back to haunt them. Think back and ask yourself a few questions…

When did you stop listening? Why did they/you stop listening?

Why and how can you turn your back on the sacrifice of your Mom, Dad, and your Family?

Was it family first or stupidity first?

Did you listen first, or ignore first?

Did you show respect first or disrespect first?

"OVERCOME" Words for YOU

Did you fix yourself or did lose yourself?
Did you talk it out or did you scream it out?
Did you smooth it out or did you shoot it out?
Did you hug and kiss, or did you swing and miss?

What happened?
Why, When, How did it get to this?
<u>When did you become blind to common sense?</u>

Back to graduation day...Graduation Day is a big celebration for you... On a scale on 1-10 Graduation day is about a ten (10) for you. Your family is there, but what you don't understand is that you think graduation day is for you. It really isn't about you at all ...It is about your parents and your family. On a scale of 1 to 10 it's a hundred (100) for the women that carried you into this world...

As you walk across that stage, she is thinking about the time you learn to ride a bike, she is thinking about the first birthday card that you drew and she proudly hung on the fridge. She even remembers the first time you said I love you Mom. She is thinking about the first Easter egg hunt, and how you were so afraid of the person in the rabbit suit. As the announcer called your name graduation day, she screamed inside the name of Jesus (Thank you Jesus!). She's grateful to all of your helpers along the way.

Today you are receiving your diploma, but your Mother is receiving so much more…

She is receiving his gift of answered prayers.

She understands that if not for God's protecting hand, instead of a diploma in a basket she's grateful not to have received a young body in a casket…Grateful for your survival and success. Your mothers sacrifice deserves this day…
Your grandmother's prayers deserves this day. Your family and teachers that saw your greatness, even when you denied them, deserves this day… This is your opportunity to repay …

The greatest compliment a boy or girl can receive is when someone asked "Who Raised That Boy?"
"I would like to meet your Mother and Grandmother"

"OVERCOME" Words for YOU

"Change for a Change"

Today I'm going to share a conversation that I have with a homeless man I met at a gas station. What he describe was very honest and helpful to me as I used that conversation to motivate a CHANGE

One day I stopped at the corner store to purchase gas. As I was pumping gas, a homeless man approached me. He asked me for some spare change. I took advantage of the moment and began a conversation with him. He was uncomfortable at first and seemed to want to rush away. Did you ever imagine this situation could happen to you I asked?
As he began to talk about his life, I discovered many of the qualities and characteristics that he had were similar to many of you sitting here today. He was one that was not able to let things go. He described himself as a person that wanted to win every argument. He was the type of person that was unwilling to listen to his parents. He even expressed regret that he was a person that wanted to experience adult situations before as a teenager. He confessed that he disrespected his elders; he frustrated teachers, and anyone that simply wanted to help him. He

began drinking alcohol and smoking at an early age. He was a person that trusted no one.

I encouraged him to CHANGE. "Change for a Change" I explained. It's never too late to become a better you. Then we continued the conversation about what he was like when he was young.

Some of you may enjoy fighting for immature reasons that have nothing to do with your success. Then I noticed his pregnant friend peeking from behind the ice machine; my heart began to wonder about the future of the baby (star) jailed in her stomach… A baby imprisoned before birth in her stomach for its protection, only to be imprisoned after birth for our protection. Many would agree with this but I say to you today, that does not have to be the case. That child can be the one that will lead you to the light.

**The word INSIGNIFICANT should forever be removed from the English Language…
Everyone matters…**

"Unfortunate Beds makes Brilliant Heads"
"Tragedy Can Be the Birth of Greatness"
"Tragic moments can change you for the better"

"God will give you change for a change"

"Tragedy is Personal, but it's not a personal attack"

Respect All Women

Start changing today...Its easy to respect women... A woman will carry the boy that is destined to become a Man... A woman will carry him for 9 months in most cases. The closest to death a woman experience is when giving birth to a child. A woman brought us into this world. A woman made the ultimate sacrifice for you to arrive at your destination. That is a debt that as a boy you must always strive to pay off. Respect all women because of their greatness of Life...Respect all women because of their sacrifice from the beginning... actually before you're beginning... A woman carried you 6,7,8,9 months...I'm sure it wasn't a cake walk...

"Don't blame her! Fix yourself Sir"!
Adversity is universal and so is achievement. No matter the situation there is hope. Don't let go of the rope. Hold on and just survive.

Today I speak to motivate you and remind you, the struggle is real but temporary.

But

"We Can, We Will, We Must!!!
OVERCOME

"Shut Up and Get Busy"

I often discuss with young people from tough environments and remind them that someone else has a tougher or worse situation than their own current predicament.

I often see young folks playing the victim card. They are distracted, empty, or feeling sorry for themselves, because of their current situation. Sometimes you need a wakeup call; you need someone to care enough to deliver tough words, and the tough love to help you overcome tough times.

It takes courage to look at a love one and express to them that they are dead wrong at a time when they are hurting or going through anguish. My Grandmother always told me two wrongs don't ever make a right. If a wrong is witnessed, it is our duty to declare the truth (especially family). This is not as difficult if you are dealing with a stranger. There are no emotional ties, but when it comes to our own family that has made poor decisions landing them on <u>their last leg</u>. How brave will you be? Will you have the courage? Will you be afraid to deliver the final blow of tough love?

The final blow can be the beginning of the "New Show". You have nothing to lose and everything to gain. A change must happen today.

"Shut up and Get Busy" it's time to be fixed with help.

"You want us to see, hear, and feel your EXCUSE rather than see your USE".

"The Chair"

Today's message is for all the youngsters out there that has lost a father, don't know their father, never met their father, or saw him jet...

You got to hold on. You got to fight for your right to find happiness. Your family need for you to step up...The empty CHAIR will not always be empty...Your father CAN'T be replaced, but the empty chair can...

You must fill the CHAIR with your body and his air... You must breathe for him. You must hold the hands of his granddaughters and grandsons... You must also hold your Mom's hand.

You have the responsibility to move on and close the emptiness of others. As you close the emptiness of others, you will then become full...You have the responsibility to share more, to care more... Moving on does not mean you're over his lost...It simply means that you are moving forward and taking his lost with you...

Young Fella you got to fill the CHAIR with pride and love, either the pride and love he left you with or the pride and love you had to discover for yourself…

Your father's loss or sacrifice, no matter if it was due to negligence, or if it was due to a courageous battle…You must mark your sacrifice to be more than his…because that the way life is… Each generation improves the next generation…

You learn more from losing or overcoming tragedy than you'll ever learn from winning… You become stronger after you've overcome some tragedies in your life…Your fathers lost past or his precious pass has paved the path for your Greatness.

The CHAIR is no longer empty…although it's full of the lost memories, regrets, and sacrifices. The CHAIR is also full of your future hopes, your futures dreams.

You now must grab ahold of the lonely hands that's missing him…You must demonstrate love to the ones he loved or the ones he should have loved…You must be responsible, you must care, and you must share…

"OVERCOME" Words for YOU

You must share his lost but also you must share your find…You've found his spirit and you've found your spirit also…it's a part of you…

You must sit in the empty CHAIR starting today. Man up now young Fella. The CHAIR is no longer empty if you "Got his Back"… Say it… "Things were not perfect but must have Your Back"…. "I must have our families Back"

As I sit in the CHAIR today Dad… Remember although I'm sitting in the CHAIR, always remember that I'm standing up for what you started, no excuses even if your presence was not what it needed to be, I must build for a better next generation… Coach Bruce Etheridge

PS…Now sit up straight…Pull up you pants, and "Shut up and Get Busy"…

> "Sometimes the strongest Men can only bench press a few pounds…The measure of a Man or Husband is not in his physical strength.
>
> Simply look at his Words and Deeds then notice the emotional weight lifted off his wife and children"

The Word
INSIGNIFICANT

**Should forever be removed
From the English Language!!!
Everyone Matters!**

It's Your Passion

Not Your Position

"OVERCOME" Words for YOU

Running for "The Answer"

At 10 you're **running** everywhere…no worries…
At 15 you're **running** to find yourself…

At 20 you're **running** searching to find it…
At 25 it finds you and you think of **running** away…

At 30 your **running** slows to find a mate and you began to wonder   about the ANSWER…

At 35 you're **running** with your mate to keep up with the children..

At 40 slowly **running**, you begin to wonder "is time running out"?
At 45 you begin **running** away from silliness toward seriousness..

At 50 you're desperately **running** and to find the **ANSWER**
At 55 your new **ANSWER** finds you and the **ANSWER** begins **running** your life..

At 60 you are relentlessly **running**, telling others of the **ANSWER**
At 65 you're **running** towards the **ANSWER's** gated community…

At 70 you ask the **ANSWER** was my **running** enough? What else can I do?
At 75 you share your victory of **running**, so others will run also…

At 80 you're **running** as if you're 10 years old, no worries………**"Once a Man Twice a Child"**

Some find the ANSWER earlier in life… the sooner the better…but once you find the ANSWER… The **Answer** will save you, your family, your lost son, your pregnant daughter, the abused mother, help you get a job, deliver a unexpected blessing… the ANSWER will guide you to the lost, have you speak for the muted, have you feed the hungry, and have you giving the living water to those that are thirsty…

The ANSWER will awaken your soul and allow you to enjoy your life of RUNNING…

> *Muhammad Ali said*
> *"A Man who views the world at fifty, the same as he did at twenty, has wasting thirty years of his life"*

"OVERCOME" Words for YOU

"Lock Your Faith"

"Your test today to checkmate who you are"

As I speak on this subject today, I find many verses from the poem "Test Day" intriguing and could be great speech starters. "I must know who I am and not allow bitterness to change me". We should be able to describe the positive qualities that we have and that we see in others. You may be kind or you may be generous, or you may be unselfish, or you may be tender hearted

One day in class we decided to celebrate the positive characteristic of our class. I brought a dozen of doughnuts, twelve juice cups to drink, and twelve bags of chips. We only had twelve students in the class so each student would be able to get one doughnut, one drink, and a bag of chips each. I then added another student to the mix because I wanted to see how the good students would handle the situation. As the students listened to the soft relaxing piano music, my helpers began to issue a plate to each student. After a few moments a joyous time became a sinister time for a couple of the students as they began to argue about who deserves the drinks and snacks.

The students allowed the situation to change who they were. It was a great teaching moment for me. We shared the importance of knowing who we are, also locking in on who we would like to be. We discussed the importance of keeping our core values even in tough, unfair situations. This is very difficult to do if not practiced. The question I posed to those students was **"do tough situations change tough people or do tough people change tough situations"**.

"Stay in check today, in me the KEY, I must lock my FAITH"

We know the keys to our lives, our hearts, and keys to a quality life. We must also protect the keys, so in essences put a lock on the lock…I am the Key to protect my valuables. What's in your heart is valuable. The thief of the night will try to steal your heart or harden you beyond repair. ***Protect Your Valuables…***
The thief will try to steal you kindness, generosity, your unselfishness.

I'm not a victim!!!

You're not a victim!!!

I'm not a Lie!!!

You're not a Lie!!!

I'm a Fact!!!

You're a Fact!!!

I'm BLESSED…You're Turn…

Season Angels...

Sometimes friends (Season Angels) come into your life for a period of time that's right for you. After a mix-up or disagreement an entire friendship seems to become a waste.

Come on Man!!!

God has sent you someone (a season angel) to get you through a tough period and this is how you thank God with bitterness and regret... Although that (season angel) friend may have helped you overcome life's other tragedies such as divorce, death, a lost job, or a financial emergency.

Come on Man!!!

God will send season angels into your life at the right time. That does not constitute that they must remain in your life forever. Someone else may need them as you did in your time in need...We must appreciate the seasons and move on without strife or anger.

"I must know who I am and not allow bitterness to change ME"

Racisim

The tragedy of racism is not that a race has been dissed;
The bigger tragedy is the opportunities that will be missed.

If grand opportunities others receive are never there
Bitterness, distrust, and anger will multiply;
the "cupboard of life" will soon become bare.

If financial growth has a minimum cap,
Minimum wages, minimum opportunities will increase the gap.

Education the key to close financial gaps
College will have to be discounted or free
because our wallet has already been capped.

Those that do not attend college,
Are their opportunities hopeless dreams?
They deserve a piece of the American pie
Good jobs, great vacations too it seems

If the judicial system continue to penalize at a higher rate,

The steel silver hand cuffs will cuff the hated wrist more without debate.

If education, work ethic, spiritual and financial growth are the keys to success Then the path of racism can only slow not stop, a fact we can all attest.

If we truly, truly understand this Then we must recognize its dangers and <u>"Overcome"</u> this list.

Why do you want anyone to see your excuse? You should want everyone to see your use. No Excuses...Produces!

Fight Racism!

OVERCOME
Words for You

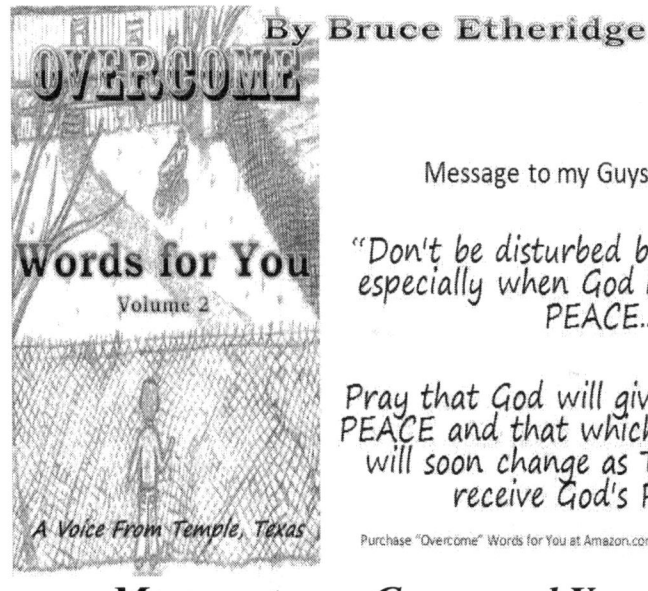

By Bruce Etheridge

Message to my Guys...and You...

"Don't be disturbed by others anger especially when God has given YOU PEACE...

Pray that God will give the angry one PEACE and that which angered them will soon change as THEY begin to receive God's PEACE"

"OVERCOME" Words for YOU

How do you want to be REMEMBERED?

Get Ready!!! Get Set!!! GO!!!

"Fruit hanging from a Tree"…
        Signaled we must CLIMB the tree for justice

Sitting at a counter…
        Signaled we must STAND at the counter for justice.

Riding in the back of a bus…
        Signaled we must DRIVE forward for justice…

A peaceful walk in Selma…
        Signaled we must RUN everywhere for justice…

Outrageous shootings and blaming fear of blackness…
        Signaled we must FIGHT legislation for justice…

FEAR of a toy gun, a can of tea, a knife walking away.
        Signaled our BATTLE for protection and for justice

We don't need any more SIGNALS

We can't SIT STILL OR KEEP SILENT, relying on introverted thoughts, voiceless facial gestures while injustice is roaming the nation. We can't continue to BELIEVE and HOPE for a change. We must pay to make change happen…

"SILENCE will never force CHANGE
SILENCE only serves to MAINTAIN"

    Rubber bullets, water hoses their aim that day
    Forever BITTER and ANGRY to be treated that way

Loud speakers, Billy sticks, the bites of dogs
Didn't soften our FLESH, We survived it all

Bruises, spit, and even tar upon our FACE
Couldn't disfigure our pride or dirty our RACE

Young fruit hanging after dark, his dreams they attempted to destroy
Strengthen our RACE and determination…NEVER TO FORGET THE SACRIFICED BOY

Sitting in the Bus, forced to the back…
She refused, we recovered never loosing TRACK

A RACE sitting down and refusing to leave the counter
Their refusal changed the moment, they changed the PARAMETERS

Shot in the back because of made up fear…
Time's up Boss! Not another TEAR!!!

Fear of the front so he was 5x shot in the back…
Is it time for me to get a GUN for such a cowardly act?

Our Savior recognized his palms reaching high to the sky
Enrage our anger, our frustration, and our conscience, damn another tearless CRY

Good people, good parents, even college students, now bigots with Guns?
Racism fueled… Americans and religions confused…
Wearing vest and using bombs…

Living in America tougher than you THINK
Time for Real change before AMERICA sinks…

The ugly pattern started long ago without care,
A mumble at first…and then a false white stare

The mumble became a whisper, the whisper became a yell

"OVERCOME" Words for YOU

The yell so loud, the nation refused to acknowledge the BELL

After the yell, then came the real fight.
Hate, fear, and revenge clashing
Both side determined to be right.

The battle continues, death wounds, and battle scars.
Today we are caught in a hate, and not so civil War!

America you say trust the system…trust the system?
Trust a system that requires INNOCENCE to be double victims…

In America…Guns loaded with lead…In Flint water full of lead…Now in America…children and parents living with lead False apologies always follow…led by craziness…Oh God! I'm shaking my head…

A system that lacks of opportunity, entrenched by profits and greed to the core…
Now the new lynching rope made of lead and water to drink or pour…

Their new racism is not an attack the black race…
But to cut cost, ignore the poor and poison their space.

Times are a changing but history is repeating the scary pattern…
Dear God, where are you? Our darkness needs your precious lantern…

We must meet face to face, not race vs. race…
America's memory and history presents a sad dangerous case…

"Where there is no struggle, there is no progress" –MLK

© "Overcome Words for You" by Bruce Etheridge ©

Father Needed

I have the tools

I have the determination

*I have my teachers on my side
and hopefully family.
But if not, so what…*

No Excuses Produces!

YOUR GREAT...HE'S LATE!

*When the boy was ten years old his
Favorite Super Hero was Superman...
Then Batman...Then Spiderman.....*
<u>*Then he met his Father*</u>

"OVERCOME" Words for YOU

It's Your Passion!!! Not Your Position!!!

Don't allow your position to limit your passion of helping others; nor limit your passion of guiding others in the right direction. The key components in every school are good teachers, good principals and quality administrations. These components are imperative for a good education. But the best educators of life come from all corners of a successful school. Many times the best difference makers in schools come from the most surprising positions.
In many schools the most important employees are those that receive little compensation or acknowledgement. I mention this because one day as I was speaking to my wife about the good old days of middles school and she began to talk about Mr. Ben (the schools custodian).   I was so amazed of her joy of him that it reminded me of the impact of a smile, a helping hand, and a protective voice in your time of need. We all have had individuals such a Mr. Ben during our educational journey…

The custodian that sweeps the floors sees it all and always protects the unprotected child from bullies. (Thanks Mr. Ben, Mrs. Rosa, Ms. Mary)

The lunch room monitor or recess monitor that commands that everyone respect the rules of order so that children can eat, play, and have fun with order. (Thanks Ms. Taplin)

The school nurse that not only takes care of the scrapes and bruises of the physical education class but also patches up the emotional scars left

The bus drivers that waited the extra time for you to arrive to catch the bus because he knew your parents needed you on that bus.

The school secretary that notices the routinely absentee child who's parent continues to oversleep or calls in multiple frivolous excuses. (Thanks Ms. Janie)

The (IA) instructional assistants, that taught you much more than the basic math facts. This person never gave up on you no matter how much you forgot the previous day's math facts. The unlimited encouragement provided daily that you so desperately needed at that moment in your life. (Thanks Mr. Trevino, Ms. Charlene)

That van owning parent that hauled all of everybody else's children to their games, practices, and school events without ever asking for gas money. (Thanks Mama Myrt)

Who was your "It's Your Passion" Difference Maker?
Who is your Difference Maker today?
Write their name down in the space provide. Let the world know…
Name_____
Name_____
Name_____
Name_____

Respect the Man of the House...

I often discuss with young boys and girls of single parents;
"If you don't live with your Daddy or don't know him, then it really doesn't matter"
What's important is that you know who YOU are! You have the biggest influence on you!!!

Respect the Man of the House!

Children will recognize the mate with a good heart. Don't run them off because he or she may not be your biological Father or Mother. Your Mom deserves to be happy with the time she has left. Leave the scars of your past, your scars of bitterness, your scars of the missing parent in the past. You are not responsible for your parent's burdens, don't judge them. Fix Yourself!!!

Your mother deserves and should have happiness in the future. I remind you today to search for your Mom's happiness of the future rather than your bitterness of the past. Live better; be better for the todays and the tomorrows in spite of your yesterdays. **"Don't Run Him Off"**

PASSION

Coaches exudes passion every day by their commitment to details for individuals to improve ... ability to show compassion in moments of distraction... ability to not allow stressful moments invade teaching moments... firmness to do what's right, in wrong moments...

That's "PASSION"...Passion and leadership is recognized by those you teach and reach, not by books, definitions, or awards...

"OVERCOME" Words for YOU

"My Diary"

(The diary of the fatherless teenage girl)

Dear Diary,

I need my Father. I never met him but I believe him to be a good man. My mom says different, but she seems very angry and bitter. I'm in school now and I see all the other students with their dads. Dads and Daughters are walking the same halls that I walk, sitting in the same class room that I sit in... What happened? I have no one to hold my hand. I'm nervous, the boys are looking at me as I try not to be seen. It seems everyone is invisible except for me. A little boy pulled my hair, another one laughed at the stains on my shoe. My mother preregisterd me for school last week so today (the first day of school) I'm on my own to discover the swirl instead of discovering the world. I'm alone, I feel alone, I see the loneliness of the world with two eyes, but both eyes belong to me, not my father.

Where is he? The world is so cold...I feel a need to always wear a jacket. Even in the spring and summer, I feel the need to wear my jacket. Is it to protect me from the cold cruel world. As I lie in my bed at night I dream of my father's warmth. I know he is out their looking for me, so as soon as I turn thirteen I will run away to find him. I may have to enlist the help of others to maintain my lifelong search. I will ask some of the boys to help me. I will befriend them so that one day I will see the Man (my Dad) of my dreams.

My Knight (Dad) in shining armor will save me some day. He will make up for all that was lost when I was a child. The journey will have taken a tremendous toll on me and my body. But when I find him in the end, it will be worth the expensive cost of my voyage.

      During my journey I will face many obstacles. I will fight the other girls whose Dad's were there for them, because they looked down on me. My journey will demand that I spend the night in the streets and maybe sleeping in boxes during my search. My journey will demand that I sleep or spend the night at some of those mean boys houses so that they can rest on me. They will need rest and energy for our journey to find my father. Oh I'm so happy to depend on those mean boys to join me in my painful journey, they seem so noble now. My mom gave up on the search a long time ago. I can't wait to tell my Dad about my long journey to find him and of my sacrifices to find him. I'm sure my dad will ask me about the scar on my neck.

"OVERCOME" Words for YOU

You see, I had to sleep in the streets for a while. A drunk old man cut me as he attempted to cut my shorts off. It was my fault though because I think I startled him as he slept next to me in the box. Someone said he was an old thug soldier of the streets. It's okay because he was a soldier I guess. Thug soldiers are good people aren't they? I've been rushed to the hospital a couple of times because of a feverish cold. I don't understand why I"m so sick. My friends continue to give me pills from their parents medicine cabinet to make me feel better.

Thank goodness for the pills because they allow me to rest anywhere and dream of you Daddy. Mom don't understand me Dad. She keep saying that you are low down good for nothing. I know that's not true and together you and I will prove her wrong. I will never stop looking for you Daddy. By the way, I'm sorry for quiting school, but I just didn't have time for that. Finding you is too important. I can't waste the little time we have left once I find you Dad. I'm sure you will be so happy to see me, and soon your new family will accept me and we will live happily ever after.

Dear God, How did I get here? Someone told me my Dad is here today. A voice whispered "It is time for you to see your Father". But everything seems so calm, so peaceful. I hear the trumphets blazing. The brightest lights I've ever seen are shinning on me. Wow, my Dad has prepared a surprise Birthday party for me. Wow, my endless journey is about to be finally over. Today, my father will welcomed me into his home. Then a beautiful voice said to me "My Child, I could not wait any longer, today I have finally claimed you...Today, you have finally found me. God is that you?...What happened? As you searched for your Dad, I, your Father, searched for you my child. Welcome home my child...

A Girl without a Father will search farther and farther to find her Father...
She will search, find, an accept an empty Man without a plan
Because her Father wasn't there to teach her to take a stand...
Today I stand, determined to take a stand and to make good choices

Girls must be prepared...This is the quote used to motivate fatherless daughters... great girls... Girls and Boys must be reminded to define their own greatness. Don't adopt the weakness or excuse of the missing parent...

YOUR GREAT...HE'S LATE !

"OVERCOME" Words for YOU

You Belong Here

Hello... You're a wonderful Girl
Confusion and Insecurity just happens to rule your world

Hang in there, you're okay,
Don't confuse your Song
Your life is important, your mind is wrong

Todays filled with anger, bitterness, and gloom
Your skies appear to be foggy and gray

Tomorrows powerful rays from God brings
Better decisions to enlighten your way

Control your emotions, there is no excuse!
Refuse the excuse, allow other to see you use

Goodbye... you had so much potential
Confusion and insecurities I guess, too detrimental

Why, why, why, all the questions we cry
Why did you give up? Why did you leave?
Why did you have to die?

You should have hung in there!
We screamed, we cared, and we loved you!
Remembering sadden and angry clouds
Painful skies are never blue

Today, I stand before a casket,
Listening to a sad piano song
Life cut short, too impatient,

Rough seas eventually calm
No pain, anger, nor gloom, all has past,
Riding with Angels to face the Mighty one,
Life judged by God, his judgment at last...

Emotions under control now, no excuse needed there
You're with the Almighty, His hand will always care

His understanding HANDS always recognizes what to do
Today's verdict of his court, commands you to start anew

Your life lost due to a self-inflicted attack
Now, you have a tan of gold, how did you come back?

Stop the presses... Stop the presses...
A reward for the bended knees
The verdict, only he understands and blesses

Where did you come from?
A rewarded for our prayers I guess
Thank for returning our friend, God knows what's best

Hello... we meet again today
The Almighty returned you my friend
So I must say hang in there, don't confuse your song

Your life is important, your mind was wrong...

What Does A Hero Look Like?

What does a Hero look like? Hero's look like YOU! **I remember a story of a misunderstood boy**...A boy in the hoodie that gave his life to save a life. As another boy was drowning in the river, everyone was standing around waiting for someone to save the drowning kid.

While others hesitated, the troubled boy, the hoodie wearing boy, the misunderstood boy dove into the raging water without fear...

"You Get What You Give in life
Tragedy can be the Birth of Greatness"

Where did his bravery come from? Maybe from the 28 hours of labor his single parenting mother went thru to deliver him into the world...The struggle that delivered him into this world...Was that the key to his bravery...

Did his mother plant in him the courage?
Did she plant in him the gift of becoming a hero?
  Did she plant his determination to hold on to save the drowning boy without letting go...?

Her sacrifice at his birth was for his sacrifice that day. His Mother's sacrifice was the life jacket he needed to swim into the river of everlasting lasting Life, the world of Eternity…**Because** of his sacrifice to save someone else's life… He became the Man that she planted in him at his BIRTH.   His purpose was served…

Question-What's your purpose today? What's your sacrifice today? What's planted in you? **You** must look inside of yourself and see if you can find someone's sacrifice…You must look inside and see if you can find someone's courage. **You** must look inside to see if you can find someone's bravery…YOU must look inside and see if you can find someone that you can trust anytime, anywhere, anyhow…

There are no excuses for you!
Your life is not the fault of anyone…Your life is a path of improving you and the path to where you want to go… Just say this today right now…I have the tools, I have the determination, and I have my teachers on my side…and hopefully family, but if not so what…NO EXCUSES PRODUCES…

Failure = Success

As you grow older from time to time, life will surprise you with a setback of some kind. **Today's message is very important and one that you must know and understand... Failure is the biggest contributor of Success.** Let me say that one again...**Failure is the biggest contributor of Success...**

"If you get fired on the job...it can lead to a new and better job for you...It can lead to more freedom for you, it can lead better hours for you, and it can even lead to better pay..."

"If you fail to get a raise, or fail to get a promotion, or fail to get the scholarship you wanted or needed. You can come back stronger, smarter, and sharper in the near future...You can improve yourself to become better prepared...Bounce back from failure...

That's what life is about, bouncing back from adversity with renewed vigor, renewed focus, and renewed determination. I'm sure this makes sense to you as we speak of its logic without strife in your life...

But when strife arises in our life...Oh oh!!! That's the point when bouncing back becomes a bounce attack. Our spirit has been attacked, our confidence, even our vision of success is under attack... Now check this one out... *Jesus was attacked so you can bounce back. His flesh, his spirit, his vision for you, all came under attack. He bounced back for you to become a successful in all your endeavors. Can you bounce back from a failing marriage or relationship? Failure in a relationships or marriage does not mean that you are a failure in life... Jesus wants you to be a successful father or mother.*

A bad marriage or a home with constant fighting can distract the parents from their responsibilities to their children.

If you have a failed relationship or marriage... can it lead to you becoming a better Daddy or Mother? It can if you get your priorities straight...You can have more freedom with your children, you can have better quality hours with your children, you can be better for your children. A Failed marriage or relationship does not mean that you are a failure in life…

As a matter of fact it may only means that it's time for you to get right…Get yourself right… "Failure is the greatest contribution to success"…Quit feeling all is lost…it's time to fight for your life, fight for your success, fight for your children's happiness and interest…

I read somewhere that "Happiness starts with you," not with your relationships, not with your job, not with your money, but with you. Your family needs for you to get your stuff together, find your greatness and happiness…

Your grandmother is watching… Your mothers is watching…You X may be watching also…Who cares…But you know what…Your children are watching and waiting…YOU should not be watching, waiting and procrastinating, but you should be elevating because God's watching and dictating… He's got his pencil out and taking note…

"Failure can be the biggest contributor of YOUR Success"

Race-Time-Choice

Is it a race against time or a time against race?
Why do we charge the poor a more expensive space?

People need help, it's no crime.
Like farmers needing subsidies it's the same welfare line.

People are tired and hungry; their food has lost its taste.
While the politician's line their pockets and vacation at a more relaxed pace.

Education, is the leveling Key?
A key made of Gold, too expensive for me.

Clothing, food, and water all too much lost.
While politicians, don't even know what a gallon of milk cost.

A race based on race is a race that's difficult to run.
But, a race racing forward is a race already won.

Timing of time is important all the time.
If the times aren't timed, hard times will be multiplied times when the good times are mine.

Choose chosen if choice was your choice to be,
Chosen is the choice that chooses yourself you see.
Is it Choice? Is it Time? Is it Race?

It's cool though, is it race against time,
Or is it time against race
That's on my mind.

OWNERSHIP

I start today by telling you a story of a very, very rich Man. Although he was rich, he was sort of a lonely Man that traveled the world in search of happiness… He traveled to Europe, Africa, China, and many other places searching for happiness, companionship, friendship…

After his long journey of traveling, searching to find the ANSWER, he returned home a sad, lonely, and depressed man… I hope that's not you today… Some of you may be sad, lonely, confused, depressed or you may know of someone who's feeling that way… You may be searching for happiness in the wrong places or they may be searching in the wrong places…

I also know of a poor, very poor Man … The poor man didn't own but few pair of pants…a couple of shirts…and his bank account totaled the maximum amount of coins that his banking jar could hold… Although the poor man never left his home to go any other place, he was happy, compassionate, and he seem to have a little light burning inside of him. He was a Man that smiled all the time.

The rich man traveled the world in search of happiness…and never found it… The poor Man never left his hometown and lived in happiness. The key to "rich Man's sadness was not in the distance that he traveled but in the distance he did not travel. The key to "Poor Man's happiness wasn't the distance he didn't travel, but in the distance he did travel.

You see the poor man's knees traveled twenty-four inches to the floor and he found a lifetime of happiness. His knees traveled to the floor and he gained the World. The short distance of your knees traveling to the floor and you too will gain your happiness. I hope that to be you today. You see the poor man was rich… and the rich man was poor. The poor rich Man… He OWNED his salvation… While the rich poor man only RENTED his salvation…

I ask you today are you an OWNER of your salvation or are you a RENTER of your salvation…Sometimes the "Rent to Own" method is good for buying worldly things but NOT when it comes to your <u>SALVATION</u>. Are you an OWNER of your salvation, or a RENTER? If you know you are an OWNER…You can praise him right now and lift your hands to the sky and thank Jesus if you are….
Renters… if you are a RENTER of your salvation then go to the closet and bend your knees and ask Jesus to save you…if you want to do that right now I got time… Ask Jesus to grant you the ownership papers for your salvation.

Some sitting here today have pain in your life because of a lack of exercise…lack of bending, lack of praying, lack of serving him, or lack of

living by his rules. Your Salvation has nothing to do with living a perfect life, but consistent moments of bending your knees, consistent moments of prayer and serving humanity, and consistency to his word, God will reward you.
LET ME SAY THAT ONE AGAIN...
Your Salvation has nothing to do with YOU living a perfect life, but consistent moments of bending your knees, consistent moments of prayer and serving humanity, and consistency to his word is the KEY…

Life is full of test. You will be tested but today I must remind you that the GREATEST grader of test will judge your answers. Jesus will be the scantron that will grade you and grade your life…
LET ME SAY THAT ONE AGAIN...

Today, God's has many messages for you. But the main message is about you having OWNERSHIP of your SALVATION. Don't run AWAY because you're not perfect…Run to Him because he is PERFECT…He is perfect for you, he is perfect for your children…he is perfect for your problems…He is the FIXER…He is the ANSWER…

Forgive to Live

I remember the time we lost a big playoff basketball game. As a coach I was devastated because I felt my team lost because I had been out coached... ***The thing that gave them an edge was that they knew our coaches off the court personalities...*** We knew nothing of their coaches off the court personalities... As the game came down to the final two plays we failed to stop their game winning play...Then it was their time to stop our game winning play and they did... We lost and I was devastated for letting the championship get away... I was out coached...I was embarrassed, I was ashamed to face my players the next day...I was very low and feeling sorry for the situation... Leaders, accept responsibility, evaluate, and devise a plan of change. The next day as I began to prepare for season ending speech I struggled to face the guys (especially the seniors). I had failed them...I struggled to pick myself up and go to the locker room to talk to them...

I'm sorry, I failed you, I was out coached last night. Please forgive me I'm very sorry for the seniors on this team... You've invested so much...you believed in me so much I feel horrendous right now...it was my fault, it was my mistake, I fell short in my preparation...

The room remained quiet for 3 minutes (it felt like Hours), as the players digested what I had just confessed... **"*it's okay coach we will get them next year*"**. The players began to talk among themselves and offered situations that occurred in the game that may have also contributed to our loss... I realize how valuable forgiveness was that day... Sometimes we must be able to forgive ourselves in order to move forward. Forgiving others will give you the strength to get back up, to carry on, and to rejuvenate your efforts, to get up and trust again... I promise the graduating seniors the championship that had eluded them. We went on to when two championships in the next 3 years... That success would not have happen without our family coming together, sticking it out and forgiving one another of the past failure. We must do this in our own families...Life is not perfect, we must "Forgive to Live"

As you grow older from time to time, life will surprise you with a setback of some kind. Today's message is very important and one that you must know and understand... Failure is the biggest contributor of Success... Let me say that one again...**Failure is the biggest contributor of Success...**

"If you get fired on the job…it can lead to a new and better job for you…It can lead to more freedom for you, it can lead better hours for you, and it can even lead to better pay for you". "If you fail to get a raise, or fail to get a promotion, or fail to get the scholarship you wanted or needed. You can come back stronger, smarter, and sharper in the near future…You can improve yourself to be better

That's what life is about, bouncing back from failure with renewed vigor, renewed focus, and renewed determination. I'm sure this makes sense to you as we speak of its logic without strife in your life…But when strife arises…Oh oh!!! Now check this one out… Can you bounce back from a failing marriage or relationship? Failure in a relationships or marriage does not mean that you are a failure in life…

> **A bad marriage or a home with constant fighting can distract the parents from their responsibilities to their children.**

If you have a failing relationship or marriage…can it lead to you becoming a better DADDY or MOTHER? It can IF you get your priorities straight…You can have more freedom with your children, you can have better quality hours with your children, you can be better for your children. Failure in relationships does not mean that you are a failure in life… As a matter of fact it only means that it's time for you to get right…Get yourself right… Carefully examine your contributions to the failure. Document your short comings to your maker, admit your mistakes. Don't blame others for your contribution to the sinking ship. Take ownership…Own it! "Failure is the greatest contribution to success"…Quit feeling all is lost…it's time to fight for your life, fight for your success, fight for your children's happiness and interest…

I read somewhere that *"happiness starts with you, not with your relationships, not with your job, not with your money, but with you"*. Your family will need for you to get your stuff together, accept responsibility, and find happiness…Your grandmother may be watching… Your mother may be watching…Your X may be watching also, who cares…But you know what, more importantly your children are watching and waiting on you. You had better be watching and elevating because God's watching and dictating. He's got his pencil out and taking note…

> **"YOUR Failure should be the biggest contributor of YOUR Success"**

More Motivational Poems

<u>The Poems</u> often tell a story or describe the struggle of life, crime, marriage, loneliness, romance, and many other different situations. Often arriving in the middle of the night, the writing style using common everyday language is designed make the reader feel and understand the reality of the situation. Students really enjoy the story telling motivational poems.

Message to you...
"A good heart will give in spite of being bruised... A good heart dishes out good deeds to strengthen itself... You are strengthening YOURSELF" by giving"..."Strong Men"..."Strong Women"... Come from bruises.

OVERCOME
Words for You

By Bruce Etheridge

Message to my Guys...and You...

"When I write all night I awake in the morning well rested.

Because my Soul rested as I wrote"

Purchase "Overcome" Words for You at Amazon.com

"When I write all night I awake in the morning well rested. Because my Soul rested as I wrote"

Dreams and Visions, Visions and Dreams

In a dream it seems, floating high around the room.
It's a funeral for someone that left us too soon.

The view reveals a family dressed in black.
Wait! Is that my family? Whose family is that?

In the blink of an eye,
A different view it seems to be,
A view from under the floor looking up at me

The view from the ceiling
I saw friends praying, kneeling
The lower view was of gang members
disconnected, unfeeling, upset and seething.

Friends were there to comfort my Mom.
The members were there to comfort the crime.

Friends whispered to me
And softly touched my casket
The gang members shouted
"C-Block" Get the hell out of that basket!

Friends seemed to care about my family,
Not the time.
The members concern was getting out of the
place, to go drop a dime.

"OVERCOME" Words for YOU

Friends expressed pleasures of my life
And the good times
The members expressed anger in
Getting revenge of the crime

Friends were appreciative of the Pastor,
And the words he spoke.
The members were embarrassing
And disrespecting to my folks

All hats removed, the church was packed.
The members stood out
Because they wore crooked Baseball Caps

Everyone was dressed so nice and clean.
Except the gang member's pants were sagging
at the seams.

My friend's words were so peaceful so calm
Words so touching, they calm my Mom.

The Members pointed to an empty space,
Then fingered up gang signs to enrage the
place.

Friends gathered to reminisce for a bit.
The gang members formed a circle
Bragging and rapping on their latest lick.

Friends placed pictures and flowers
On my grave
The gang members placed a bullet,
Then poured part of a 40 ounce

That they had saved…

Friend's acknowledged God,
For the gift of my life
The members moved on to continue the strife.

As I look down, I see my Mother, Family and friends.
I began to understand, I began to understand…

Another blink of the eye,
I'm now wide awake it seems.
No longer floating, it was just a dream.

My Mom voice then shouted. "Wake up Boy!
"It's time to eat, the table is set"
You've been having a NIGHTMARE
Your bed is wet!

Smiling, wet, and happy
For a second chance at life,
Saved again by my Mom's voice,
Her voice led me to the Light.

Whether or not, I was a gang member
Or a good friend
The choice is mine,
I determined the end.

Sometimes you just need family and friends…

Communicate

Express yourself, tell me what's inside!
What? Use my voice to reveal things that I want to hide?
Yes, I've told you that time and time again.
No, I rather express myself using paper and pen.

I need to know, I need to hear it.
Sorry, that voice was lost long ago in my Father's spirit.

He would never express how he truly felt.
I'm burden with the dying albatross that he dealt.

Sorry Dear, help me overcome the fear.
I want so badly for you to feel what I hear.

Question- Do you love me enough to let me go?
I love you more than you ever know.

Thanks you said it....

"Words inside a caring mind but locked away behind a muted mouth is a book full of loneliness"

Coach Etheridge

The Youngest One

The youngest of all of them
God had a bigger and better plan for him

So tall, strong, and handsome, he's the biggest one
This one's charge to be a more unselfish son

What is unselfishness? You continue to ask
The joy others receive because of the sweat from you task

When your effort can make others forget their Pain
Relying on your motivation to increase their Gain

Be proud of your Star; be proud of your Role
God's favor will multiply your bounty, ten times fold

Don't look for the reward, be the reward for the unjust
To reward the needy, your needs get BLESSED

My love for you Son, is the most unselfish love of all
The father critiques judgment daily, afraid his son will fall

When someone else's happiness bring more pleasure to you
Then someday you will become The Best Father, I know because that's what Fathers do

"OVERCOME" Words for YOU

The joy in your eyes can't compare to the joy in my soul
Your unselfish happiness completes me
My heart is solid Gold

You're the youngest, your birth order perfect as well
Perfectly learning from the others allowed you to excel

Be gracious, humble and prepare for Life's turns.
Your path includes sharp cuts and hazardous stops that arouses our concerns

You're health and safety a common worry of mine
As you go out the door,
I began to pray for you're safe return each time

Danger lurks for the dark tanned confident Man who's been trained with Strength, Pride and Joy

Remember that same Strength, Pride and Joy
Are viewed dangerously
When you refuse to be treated as a "Boy"

"Yet still Son, focus on Gods plan to lift the unfortunate as much as you can…

We must be LIFTERS, SERVERS, and SAVERS.
It's God's his command"

Amen

Why Today Coach?
(A Coaches Dedication)

Where you are today, the stay is temporary
Thus today's struggle, a place of worry

Where you are tomorrow, a grind but permanent
With bare feet, I will push you there
Upstream against the swift currents

The place I envision you tomorrow to be
The place I coach you from today you see

Today's place to be a "Stick House" of the Past
From my experience, a stick house never last

Your house today requires no pay
I must prepare the Man, my plan today
To build a house to last always

Today, I will COACH you to the BRICKS!!!
The Bricks, a place that never fall for tricks

Don't get in my way! Let me lead you today
Your Future is at stake, Let's Play then Pray

Frustration and Anger will always betray
The impatient filthy mouth of an astray

Hey, we must fix you, heal you, so LISTEN now
Dump your ashes today! Dump your ashes!
And forever leave behind the insecure glances

"OVERCOME" Words for YOU

**A clean tray, you must be cleaned!!!
Long ago your greatness was claimed,
It wasn't a DREAM**

**So your coach I am today, I will always be
The one that expects you to give more, and
expect more of thee**

**Go now, CRAWL first, and then WALK, even
sprint or RUN
Fill God's purpose for you,
"You're the Chosen One"**

**Go now, JUMP first, and then CLIMB,
Even attempt to FLY
See the WORLD, serve you purpose,
You MUST before you die**

**Yesterday you listened well;
You didn't get in my way
Now you must lead me, you must today!
Your FUTURE is secured, Let's Pray then Play**

Coach E

"I never counted my wins or losses, but I remember every victory"

PS..."Nurture their wounds past their shackles"

"Control"

If they control the narrative, they control you
If allowed that control, your future is thru
The choice of the narrative is always yours,
Don't allow anyone to close your doors

If they control your mind, they control your emotion
If allowed that control, they control the commotion
Your mind and emotions are always yours to keep,
Don't give them the shackles to control your feet

If they control the conversation,
they control what you say.
If allowed that control,
you're just a yes man and must obey

The conversation piece, is a piece of you,
no one should tell you what to say or do
The conversation is yours and speech is free,
Use your voice, the sqeeky wheel get the oil you see

If they control the time, they control your stay
If allowed that control, say Master, Master, is it okay

Time of Life, or time of day?
Keep your own watch and calendar, to avoid a delay

If they control the show, they control what you know
If they control the news, be careful it's design to confuse

Don't give them control of your mind or heart,
Control your own destination until the end
from the start

"OVERCOME" Words for YOU

It must be right whatever the time
The stongest muscle, is the muscle of the mind,

Fight for all three, your mind, heart, and your start…
Because they want you to be greatful to push a homeless cart…

Control is yours from birth till death,
It's your control until you've breathed your last breath

Control your control, to control the control, because control is control of those that think they control…

Control
Control
Control
Control
Control

My Coach

An insecure boy with low self-esteem at the time
Face oozing with pimples, an ugly duckling in my mind.

A small framed kid who felt his life was a waste.
Walked around with a permanent frown,
So people would give me my space.

My frown created a buffer
Between them and me you see.
I needed that space so that he could feel free.

Life was so unfair because my brother could not walk.
I would push him all over town,
Wheel chair bound, so we could laugh and talk.

My legs became his legs
Blessed with extra strength,
Compensating for his the stiff legs
That was permanently bent

Basketball was my life, the only true friend I had, spending every spare minute with my little round friend eased my agony of being so sad.

"OVERCOME" Words for YOU

I wasn't very talented, short, awkward, and raw.
I had a little speed and was out of control is what
the PE teacher saw.

Then the COACH entered the gym you see.
His eyes a mixture of Wildcat Blue
And Mustang Green, He was very nice to me.

Strong character and positive encouragement
He preached to a tee.
Who was this white man with green and blue eyes
that was investing in me?

Don't trust him! Don't trust him,
Raced through my mind
But his voice rang with truthfulness,
I trusted for the first time.

After years of not trusting, I finally let go,
My life flowed in ways I still remember.
Thank God for Coach Oliver
He became My Coach in late September

With pride, we would sing the school song;
Chant his favorite chant before every game.
Our unified hands along with prideful voices
honoring the Mustang name

How do you feel? He would ask three times in a row.
Alright, Alright, Alright, we would yell back to our Coach Joe.

The season soon ended with all victories
Without a hitch
Undefeated were the Mustangs, Champions *forever*
My life changed in that glitch.

Because he was my COACH I decided to be,
A coach like him to lead the lost to victory

Many years of coaching many lives we've turned.
The wins and losses not as important,
As the lessons we've learned.

He instilled and taught me;
"You Get, what you give"
Is the greatest job of all
Building relationships with people
Was OUR destined call

Sometimes in Life,
You come across a unique person you see.
Trust Him, Trust Him
He may hold the KEY…

My Coach, My Difference Maker

"OVERCOME" Words for YOU

The Forgetful Man

From time to time I forget some things,
But it doesn't mean, I'm as dumb as it seems.

Always remember that I'm a Man,
Be careful how you correct me or I'll take a stand.

I may roll my eyes in displeasure you see,
But that does not constitute that you stop helping me.

I forget some things she makes a valid case,
Women, just leave me alone and give me space.

Why do you blame me for all your short comings?
Women, my comings are not short;
It's all of your humming.

Damn, I forgot my Mom's birthday;
It's the wife's fault.
Then I sat back and thought, thought and thought.

Why am I blaming her, she didn't let me down.
It was me; it was me that's been a forgetful stupid clown.

It had to be love at first sight, now I truly believe,
Love made her stay, thank God she didn't leave.

Go buys shoes, jeans, and even a sweater.
You deserve the best, your husband will be better.

As you awake in the morning, I will have washed every dish.
I hope to reconcile my poor attitude that was completely selfish.

If you forget something I won't complain,
because you accepted the flaws of a Man insane.

My mother always told me
That one day I would see,
There is an angel out there to tolerate me.

Good Morning Angel,
My attitude adjusted and true,
Breakfast is served, the dishes has been washed,
And I won't forget to say I love you

"OVERCOME" Words for YOU

This Women

I love this woman;
Truly love this woman from now to eternity.
The longer we love each other, the better it gets for me.

I accept her, the complete woman's tears,
Even though she knows my insecurities and my fears

Disagreements and confusion in relationships are normal,
I now understand.

But the arrogance of a man won't allow him to look at his own hand.
He fears her control of his soul
Because insecurity and fear controls his mold

But her responsibility to reassure his insecurities and fears
Will only strengthen his Love of her tears

To trust this soul without worry of control is the truest love of all.
To sleep next to that women every night;
The morning brings a renewed love call.

I Love This Woman...

"If her smile doesn't make you feel good inside, then you're paying too much attention to yourself"

Half Full or Half Empty?

Is the glass half-full or is the glass half-empty?
It all depends, on the space that you live in.

Empty or Full you make the case,
Like fine wine, determined with time, is what determines your taste.

I feel so empty inside from the space you occupied, The place where I lied and could not hide.

"OVERCOME" Words for YOU

You look so full, so brilliant and so complete.
Not a hint of pain, but it's confidence I see.

Damn, you look so together, not a hair out of place.
The glass that contained you preserved your taste.

I'm upset, because I feel I deserve credit.
For preserving you and giving you the confidence to go get it.

Frustrated, embarrassed, I feel so sad because now I know it's me that taste bad.

The glass I thought, held you together,
Was the container from Alcatraz to imprison you forever...

Your life, prison and freedom, now I see, the glass contained you, and would not set you free.

Space and understanding, you provided my needs with certain.
It was important to you that I blossom without feeling threaten...

Contained and encircled to keep you from the world.
The prison cell that you dwelled not enough for my girl...

So selfish of me to imprison thee. You can't contain beauty it must be set free...

So disconnected, and ignorant of your needs,
While stupidly trying to sow my owns seeds...

I feel so empty because I tried to hide.
The heart-breaking lie, to only you I confide.

I realize now, why you look so great,
You now have space to grow to enrich your taste...

Imprisoned by the glass, our roles are reversed,
You have your freedom, I have my curse.

I'm contained in the emptiness of the glass.
You occupy the fullness that will always last.

I'm left to myself, like a lost ship at sea.
Trapped in a half-filled glass that serves to imprison me.

Live life abundantly, you've been set free,
I deserve the circular prison for what I did to thee.

Freedom, Freedom, never to be my space.
Our roles now reversed by God's good grace...

Why am I so empty, Why are you so full?
The answer revealed by a reversal tool...

My final request, one last kiss,
to remember the women that I will forever miss.

Waiting, hoping, that you'll return home.
Never trapped again, Are you forever gone?

I hope for a storm now, I need the perfect storm.
To be her hero again to protect her from harm.

Uh, Oh, there may be hope today,
the glass tilts and begins to sway,

*Wave after ripple, ripple after wave.
Lost at sea, my life needs to be saved.*

*Please God forgive me,
I know a second chance kiss is extrememly slim.
Wait, wait, I think I see see lip stick on the glass rim.*

"Words inside a caring mind but locked away behind a muted mouth is a book full of loneliness"

Coach Etheridge

"OVERCOME" Words for YOU

Birth Order

He was the first, the first to be,
A descendant of the fruit,
A descendant of the leaves

It was you; God chose your order to be.
Explore the universe, expand the family tree.

Your birth order set in stone
My hope for you to be a confident
Man once you're grown

Stay focused, your education is the key.
Don't allow hate to disrupt your exploration degree.

You must blossom because you're the first.
The second and third are watching you to reassure their thirst.

Chase the world, and find your wife to be
Send back pictures
For two and three to see

Always call home to check on your Mom,
Text me to reassure that your life is calm

The first in line is afraid to jump.
That fear is common even I got stumped.
Cash needed, just let me know

Love without judgment I willingly show

The impossibilities and insecurities you
feel, are normal for the first born.
Soon you will understand those are the
characteristics to be a strong son.

Sometimes you got lonely, because the
first born don't always get to see.
But I'm here now, I was there then,
always the leader you need.

It was then that you were ten,
You shot hoops, and then cut the yard
requesting no pay
I remember that day,
Because I saw a boy becoming a man
Surpassing me on his way

Be Proud, Patient, and Prayerful,
Always honoring the 3 P's
Also keep an eye on God and never be
afraid to speak with thee

Proud today of the order of your birth,
It's me that been blessed, because you
have validated my worth.

To my first born today I say
My hat is off to thee
Because you were the first born, the
greatest gift God could give me.

"OVERCOME" Words for YOU

Daddy's Girl

She was the first, the first Girl to be,
She's the first granddaughter, her Granny
waited so long to see.

It was you; God chose Daddy's girl to be.
Explore the universe first, and then expand
our family tree.

Your beauty like a red ruby, your birth stone
The expectations for you to be a confident,
independent woman once you're grown

Stay focused, your education is the key.
Don't allow fear or insecurity to corrupt your
beauty or your exploration degree.

You must blossom
Because you're the first girl
Many are cautiously watching you
To inspire their world

Chase the world,
Take some time to find your mate to be
Send back pictures for the family to see
damn, someone may replace me?
Hmm, well okay, but he's must have a degree
And not an ounce of jealousy

Always call home to check on your Mom,
Send me a text, I'm sending straight cash for
Daddy's girl to come home.

Restrictions, insecurities of being sheltered
are normal for a Girl
Soon you will understand those were the
protections needed in a dangerous world.

Sometimes you got frustrated,
Because you did not get a chance to see
What others saw and experienced
From their mistake laden tree

It was then that you were ten
You comb your hair to perfection that day
I think I cried, your Mom then replied,
A beautiful woman was on the way

Be Proud, Patient, and Prayerful,
Always honoring the 3 P's
Also keep an eye on God and never be afraid
to speak with thee

Proud today of the order of your birth,
It's us that been blessed, because you have
validated our worth.

To our daughter, today we again say
We will hold your hand always,
And never let it slip away

You were the first, daughter, granddaughter,
And Daddy's girl born,
Everyday seems like a Spring Christmas
Your smile is a GIFT, so beautiful and so warm

Today's Goals
(This poem inspired by my Uncle Kite)

Today's Goal is to help all that I see.
And even help those that don't request to see me.

Present them with a smile and my only request,
Use your time wisely and to do your best.

Today, I must find the sparkle in their eye.
Goal achieved, I made 50 of them smile.

Today I must make a valiant effort to match you're worth.
You are worth more than a billion according to your parents smile at Birth

Today, I must teach a child, teach a child I must, today.
Tomorrow I must reach a child, reach a child, just to say.

Hey, don't look down or don't look away
Today we smile together, like on your Birth day...

You're worth more than a Billion...

WHY AM I WRITING?

Why am I writing? What is the plan?
Is God speaking to me or is it the
frustration of a Man.

I guess it really doesn't matter.
Just ride it out and do what you feel.
Gods plan is bigger than mine
Don't worry, and just trust his deal.

I can't stop writing, words are
different but they mean the same.
Words of a common Man,
And words that God claimed.
Amen

Alexandria's Thanksgiving Des<u>s</u>ert

The Day for a Family Feast but my stomach not hungry for meat
My mind dreaming of my Mother although there was plenty of food to eat.

I need my Mother, she's never left me this way!
My Dad gone long ago
But he will text or call on my Birthday.

It's not the same, his is just an empty space
My Mom has always been there to served in his place

My thoughts are of my Mother
The city not mine, but upstate in another

I tried to be kind because it was family time.
I was missing my Mom, the only thing on my mind.

Everyone was happy it was a time for living
My Mom and I separated, for the first time on Thanksgiving

The pain in my stomach would not share
the food and desserts, my stomach didn't care

My Granny knew of my pain, she tried to ease
I'm thankful for her, its my heart she pleased

Thanksgiving is a time for family and friends
I now understand,
My Mom is always with me, and her love shall never end.

She's away to make more sacrifices for me
I got to make it through to see her face,
I must see

I feel better now that I understand the sacrifice
My Mom loves me so much I must remember her advice

Be thankful and pray during each trying day
Sacrifice is the;
Mama Alice, Big Mama, Granny Linda, my Mama, and me... The Alexandria Way

It's okay to miss my Mother on Thanksgiving Day
I can't let a temporary situation get in the permanent Way...

I'm okay...I'm okay...

"OVERCOME" Words for YOU

I'm a Father Now
(Boy)

Today my life changed I fathered a Son.
A fatherless Father,
Now responsible for this young one

Being a fatherless Father raised my expectation,
because a Son 'less Man
Tried to paved a path for my damnation

I'm here Son, never will I leave you.
My responsibilities a perfect fit like Jordan's tennis shoe.

Perfect you are for all to see.
I'm not as perfect, but you do resemble me.

What do I do now? My road was unpaved.
I will create a new path; your path will be saved.

Afraid I am, unsure of what must I do,
To protect your life from my clouded view

God I need you now more than ever.
Guide me; Guide me, what an amazing treasure.

A vision he must have, unclouded by that invisible man.
Bless him with extra senses and intuition so he can boldly stand.

A lesson taught is better than a lesson bought.
Inexperience mistakes are the only mistakes I sought.

Today my life changed, I fathered a Son.
A fatherless Father, responsible for this young one

I'm a Father Now
(Girl)

Today my life changed I fathered a child.
A fatherless Father,
Now responsible for HER young Smile

Being a fatherless Father raised my expectation,
because a Son 'less Man
Tried paved a path for my damnation

I'm here baby girl, never will I leave you.
My responsibilities a perfect fit like Cinderella's shoe.

Perfect you are for all to see.
I'm not perfect, but for you I will attempt to be.
What do I do now? My road was unpaved.
With your Mom's help your path will be saved.

Afraid I am, unsure of what must I do,
To protect your life from my clouded view

God I need you now more than ever.
Guide me Guide me, what an amazing treasure.

A vision she must have,
Unclouded by that invisible man
Bless HER with extra senses and intuition
So she can boldly stand.

A lesson taught is better than a lesson bought.
Inexperience mistakes are the only mistakes I sought.

Today my life changed, I fathered a child.
A fatherless Father, responsible for HER young SMILE

"OVERCOME" Words for YOU

The Red Oak Tree

There!!! There!!! In the field, across the street,
a huge Red Oak tree proudly stands...
That was once a lost boy but now a found
man...

Fragile, angry, and selfish was the sign nailed to
me.
Forever attached to my heart a young
immature sapling of a tree.

My leaves dropped to the ground confused and
dazed.
My branches had been exposed to too much
violence, turmoil, and haze.

An Old Red Oak tree once said to me,
"My past will strengthen my future",
A fact I now can see.
So now I promise myself to listen to that tree.
That happened to be much older than me.

Scarred with initials, tic-tack-toe and other
symbols, like tattoos of life.
The old Red Oak has memories etched into him
with someone's loose pocket knife…

A puzzling carving, revealed a crossed out
heart.
Unraveling the secret that the boy was troubled
from the start…..

Today, the Red Oak tree is standing tall,
healthy and strong.
Branches are reaching high into the clear sky.
Its branches are so long.

Be thankful for the scratches and scrapes
Endured in life's illusions
The tree's only regret not appreciating the
confusion.

Look!!! In the field, across the street,
Two huge Red Oak trees proudly stand…
They were once lost boys, but survived to
become a man…

"OVERCOME" Words for YOU

She Motivated Me

She sat in the chair,
Rolling her eyes like she didn't care…

Her slump so deep, the seat held her feet.

**"How low can you go? I sarcastically ask,
After I entered the room…**
"No Mr. E that teacher is tripping way too soon!"

**Wait, have you forgot what you were taught?
"The teacher is the Boss, the classroom is his spot."**

*No but Mr. E… Math is not my game.
He's going too fast, he doesn't even explain…*

I always struggled with math. I can't add Mr. E!
**Stop right there young lady!
You're not a pity tree!**

**You add to the world every day!
You are here, that counts, somehow, someway**

*I struggle with shapes, sizes, adding and subtracting.
It's not my style.*
Okay, time to start over, show me a smile!

Now let's fix your attitude,
Remember "The Teacher is the Boss"
You must pass that class, no matter the cost.

Oh, by the way, sit up straight,
Don't slump in that chair.
You're sending a clear message that you don't care!

You're better than that! This is your space!
You add to the class just entering the place!!!

Smiling, sitting straight,
Now you're looking good,
Now that's your style.
Is my message understood?
Yes Sir...

Now let's talk about your problem in Math
*What problem? I'm good now;
It was my attitude that was bad...*

*Mr. E, can I go back to the Math room?
I'll <u>add</u> my smile and <u>subtract</u> my attitude and pass that class soon*

Wait; remember this, "The Teacher is the Boss"
Yes Sir, He's been the Boss, no matter who's lost

*But Mr. E, I've found a better Boss
That motivated my start.
You're the best teacher Mr. E
Because you fixed my heart*

"OVERCOME" Words for YOU

A Father's Tough Love

A hard, prideful, fearless MAN to all family and kin,
That combination haunted us
It contributed to his end.

Uncompromised and unrecognizing
Of the danger to be
Alcohol fogged his judgment,
And left us without its leader you see.

Our hearts was starved and hungry inside
because he didn't express LOVE
Needed for us to survive

He wasn't a bad guy that planned to escape;
He just failed us because he didn't communicate.

Speaking of love often got in his way
which bothered the hell out of us to this day

His relationship with us was not the best
because compassion and love he refuses to express

I know he loved us in his own unique way;
sometimes you just need to hear it to start a new day

His insensitive approach
I thought ruined my chances,
To become a nurturing, confident man
Without insecure glances

He was a confrontational Father
That enjoyed a rumble,

With an explosive attitude that was hardly humble.
A Boxer I became to show toughness,
Hoping to make a connection
I endured blow after blow,
Still never receiving his affection

As a young boy I didn't understand,
My Father thought he was teaching me to be a man.

I felt he didn't care because he never said,
I love you son before tucking me to bed.

I've learned, a hardened heart with hands of stone
Is not the strength that needs to be shown

A compassionate heart expressing tender loving care
Is the type of strength, we all must share

My mission now is my Family that I must prepare,
Especially the grandchildren, their greatness I declare.

I stand today, proud, recovered and strong.
Injecting emotional greatness
That stalled us for so long

My Family's legacy was in deep need of repair,
but the legacy I will leave will resolve that despair.

From the start my Father began with a hardened heart, but in the end
His son became an understanding and sensitive friend.
I salute my Father for Legacy he tried to pave,
I understand now that it's my Legacy he saved.

MT

"OVERCOME" Words for YOU

Coaches' Clause or Coaches Claws

"Coach, you can't help them if they're not here"

Teach Toughness Every Day!

BM

Open your eyes, time has come, we must take a stand.
We can't allow coaching bullies to continue to command

Allowed to hide behind the Coaches Honor Code
Oust them to society, their practice of hate exposed.

To coach is the greatest teaching position, I was told.
To coach, teach, and motivate,
A balanced women or man must unfold

It occurs everywhere volleyball, football,
Basketball and other sports too.
Coaching with moral claws to mistreats our youth
It's logical why a coach takes a moral stand
However, issues arise when
Their moral stand is not that of the common Man

Hiding behind regulations and rules
The Moral Claws inject fear and insecurity,
To those they choose

This style is good for the favorites but bad for many
It's like loaded dice, only the roller knows the enemy

Good coaches are tough, but not all tough ones
Do what they should
They attempt to build character,
But destroy the character of good

Good Coaches Build, Instill, and Give at Will

The Claws coach degrades, invades the young hearts
Then begin their terror shortly after 1st meeting start.

Coaches can command respect, be courteous and nice
The ultimate goal is for the player to reach new heights.

Physical and emotional stability both go hand in hand
Physical greatness with an emotional scar,
Develops a dangerous Man

Don't get it wrong, The Claws coach sleep well at night.
Illogical pride in their eye, permit them to fight,
Because of near-site

The Far-sighted coach, Has the best vision it seems.
Happy parents, balanced players,
Great memories, great dreams
These bad coaches steal the player's confidence,
Then hide behind the Coaches Shield
They just don't get it! They don't understand the Deal!!!

The claws coach pattern is to shake up, break up, and kick to
the curb
Creating frustration, humiliation and disheartened players
and disturbed.

Poor leadership is easy to recognize or see
The poor communications skills, it's like talking to a tree.

"OVERCOME" Words for YOU

A barrage of filthy language and unethical sound bites, done behind closed doors,
Administrators cringe, players singe
And parent's jaws drop to the floor

To treat prized possessions with such nasty regards,
It's not their child; the Claws seemed to have no Heart.

Claws coaches don't understand the teams complete needs
Personal frustration taking precedent over the Coaches Creed

If old Claws coaches train the one's that's new;
The dangerous immoral pattern will then continue

The Moral Claws must be stopped
Futures are at stake tick-tock tick-tock

To the young coaches, getting a new start
Be yourself, do what's right, follow your own,
Not someone else's hardened heart.

Your charge is to nurture Girls into Women, Boys into Men
For a successful journey you must honor and respect them
You cannot be a "Commander in Chief"
If you're a "Demander in Chief"
Great coaches lead first with players alongside.
Bad ones lead from invisible positions to deflect and hide.

"Coaches are entrusted with family jewels in tacked
The jewels should be returned
Without a permanent crack"

The Claws Coach need to be stamped REJECTED.
Removed permanently, count those infected

The Claws addressed a player's weakness
As individual sickness

The strong coach promotes the team's strengths
And understands players sometimes need to vent.

Players, parents, confused, but continue to share
Although their spirit demoralized, the Claws don't care!

They're disgracing the honorable teaching profession
Stop rewarding those teaching nightmare lessons

Good coaches are being overshadowed, it's not fair.
Parent, Fans, thought enough of you to share.

Coaches, honor your participants if you dare
I'm just an old coach that continue to CARE

"Physical and Emotional stability both go hand in hand. Physical Greatness with an emotional scar, develops a Dangerous Man"

I'm A Man

Why me, Why me, what Crime did I commit.
That made me end up in this invisible pit.

Doors locking and slamming so loud,
My mind blocks away the pain.
Rusty bolts, padded metal seat, steel frame
Screeching like a heavy train.

Legs shackled so heavy, impossible to swim to a shore
My mind imprisoned by an invisible steal door.

Phone use restricted to contact family and friends
Sometimes needing help or permission, can you imagine?

Damn, my Crime so bad that I'll never walk her down the aisle.
Never standing strong and tall beside her
To see her wedding smile

Never to go on romantic walks with her Mother
Unsure and always wondering if she will chose another.

No vacations or trips with past classmates,
My crime threatens all activities and dates.

What crime did I commit? You probably want to ask me.
I'll tell you my Crime! I was born with Cerebral Palsy.

Now is the time to break out of this rolling cell
Bring me water from your sweet well.

Gently, gently shake my hand.
I long for the gentle touch of a caring friend.

I'm a complete Man, don't pity my soul.
You're blessed with a key to help me feel whole.

Let's race. Ready, Set, Go! Walk or run?
Stop now, the race is over, I've already won

My mind has already seen the face,
And been to the place that you continue to chase

Don't look down or away. Look into my eyes.
You'll be surprise of the intelligence that belies
Let's talk, talk to me, and please don't stare.
People sometimes get distracted
Seeing the round legs on my wheel chair

Pause for a moment sit down have a seat.

"OVERCOME" Words for YOU

Drinks are on me, a Dr. Pepper my treat…

**We can talk about sports or politics if you dare
But private conversations I promise not to share.**

**Be sure to laugh or smile as you stroll by.
Even a quick nod or wink from your left eye.**

**Call, text, or email me just to say Hi.
Life's too short to ever say goodbye.**

**Parole my sentence, you've heard my case.
Join me in my world, my time, my space.**

**I have unlimited potential, only the wheel chair is restricted
A complete Man I am, I've never been convicted.**

**Thanks for understanding and visiting with me
I'm a complete Man,
Living, not dying with Cerebral Palsy**

🐎 The Greatest Cowboy 🐎

There was a great Cowboy that rode Mama, his beautiful Horse.
The real lesson the Cowboy taught us was more important of course.

The Cowboy and his Horse taught us to ride and to respect life.
Enjoy the peaks, survive the valleys, and always be nice.

Every summer his home became our family's celebration spot.
The food, the horses, the basketball court, the card games,
but the German Chocolate cake was top

He would say, stay focused, tighten your saddle, and hold on tight.
To prepare for life's ride you will need strong hands,
a good horse, and a tremendously good wife

Prepare for the tough climbs and rough times sure to come your way.
Because, **for the ride of Life**, on the Horse you must stay!

The memorable trips to his stables, our family had so much fun.
The Greatest Cowboy was our Blessing, truly our families # 1

Mama's famed prance and stubborn trot, so gentle yet so strong.
Mama's final trot, to carry the greatest Cowboy to his eternal home

Every day as the rugged clouds ride the clear blue sky
Envision him riding Mama to the Greatest Mountain, oh so high

At night as we look to the heavens, see the fullness of the Moon
Remember the GREATNESS of the Cowboy that left us too soon

His Golden Cry, "**Stick it in the Dirt**" his path for family and friends
His LEGACY, of FAMILY, of HONOR and RESPECT has no ends...

In Memory of The Greatest Cowboy--Mr. Al Taylor
He lives forever in us...

"OVERCOME" Words for YOU

"You are So Beautiful"
"Growing is Changing"

Changing is Growing, and Growing is Changing.
A taught lesson is better than a bought lesson.

Changing, Growing, learning lessons a many,
My mistakes paid for, mistakes a plenty.

I now realize I'm changing to fit,
Everyone changes… my universe demands it.

Changing, growing, and learning together
My Grandmother and Mother I will love forever,

They are my Universe I can now see.
My Universe demands that I become a better me…
Change and grow my Universe demands it.

DOCUMENT

I document visions for all to see.
For those that need love, compassion and understanding I document thee

My thoughts sometimes light, heavy, and maybe on the edge of insane,
But I've never documented, with a trace of vain.

Continue to **remember** the life lessons, conversations, and inspiration of your name.
Documented proof is not the same.

I also document silliness because silly I am.
Although silly, I'm a documented man

SACRIFICED FOR YOU

We must value our time and our life… Someone was sacrificed for you…Jesus carried your burdens, your sins, and the cross on his back… Jesus hung atop of the Cross so you wouldn't have to live on the bottom…The nightmare of his sacrifice was so that you could have great dreams not fake dreams…His faith in you was so that you could believe in him "The Son of God"… He was sacrificed so that you could have everlasting life…His spirit lives…He lives… What are you waiting for…

We've witnessed him feed the hungry…
We've witnessed him heal the sick…
We've witnessed him heal broken hearted parents of lost children…
We've witnessed him give abused women the strength to defeat their abuser…
We've seen him remove undesirable elements out of people and marriages…
We've seen him repair people, repair families and repair relationships…

Your problems is nothing compared to the victories he's already won…You are going to be a victory today…Just say these magical words…I love you Jesus…I believe in you…I believe that you died for me…I ask for your forgiveness…
Today I ask that you touch my heart with your mercy…I pray that I can serve you in some capacity… In Jesus name I confess, profess your Greatness Lord Thru you I want to share my "Story of Glory"….
Amen…Hallelujah

"OVERCOME" Words for YOU

"Missing in Action"

He was missing in action,
So action is what I found.
Filled with confusion and anger,
My wound was deep and profound.

My Heart scarred,
Anger trained me to fight.
Somehow fighting eased the painful
Memory of an abused child's life.

My Dad was abusive
And resentful of my tender Mom
He left a path of destruction,
Damn Man Come On!!!

My memories of him,
Was so unfair for a child
But when I think of my Mom,
I won, he couldn't stop my SMILE.

Family is Family abused or not,
Then one day the abuse finally stopped.

Finally, it all seemed to be over.
His luck unlucky,
By a sharpened four leaf clover

Cornered, afraid, without a choice,
Moms snap decision,
Forever erased his voice.

Family needs Family, my Mom's final prison call
Take care of my children until
I return is the price I charge y'all.

Thank God for my Mom's sister,
She helped from the start.
Mom's request answered,
My Auntie done her part

The sun will rise at some point in time
Because of Mom's sacrifice, I'll have a chance to be a better Father than mine...

There He Stood

So smooth, so compact,
So tall, so cool,
So stacked,

The Man had it all together.
From his shiny shoes to the hat with the feather

I looked at him and marveled at the site.
There he stood the Smoothest Man
I ever saw standing upright.

I gaze at him with an insecure glance.
I hoped someday to mimic his stance.

Strong, Bold, Fearless,
Describe him to a tee.
My hope was that
He would teach it all to me.

I studied his habits and his speech;
I took note during those years.
I even found a way
To even mimic his tears

He was so professional,
My mind absorbed his all.
He taught me many lessons
Beyond coaching basketball

You can't make everyone happy,
Some may fall.
Use your gift to teach life,
One day the air will leave basketball

Unbridled emotions
Can be dangerous thing
Control your emotions
Don't give anyone an excuse to sing.

God, Family first,
He conveyed every day.
The most important chapter
Taught to me in a personal way

People come into your life;
You may not understand
The reason why
But I know the reason this man did
To ensure a good father would survive.

No regrets ever stood in his way.
I admire that strength still today.

There he is again, never will he bend.
Thanks for teaching more about life,
You are a Great Friend.

Now, in my mirror,
His reflection still stands
The greatest outline of *Any Man*

Do what's required... When it's required...
And do it consistently...
-Harry Miller

"OVERCOME" Words for YOU

"Respect The Man of the House"

*A boy must respect two men in his life
Or Get out of line!*

One is the Savior, The Man from above.
Two, is the Man of the House
That taught the Boy to love

A father's role with only a few thanks,
The life this Man chose
Although not the boy's father,
He's the closest Daddy that the boy knows.

That MAN is speeding to catch up,
A role competing against himself
Not sure how to discipline the boy,
Use harsh words or a leather belt.

*A boy must respect two men in his life
Or Get out of line!*

One is Father God whose mighty book
The best seller of all-time
Two, is the "Man of the House"
Raising the boy to be "One of a Kind"

Respect Him, the "Man of the House",
For he does it all
The shopping, driving, to hauling,
And even teaching to catch the ball

Mow, fish, and even change flat tires
Fix his bike; did he teach him to use the pliers?

Every Boy must learn to fix, clean, and even cook.
For his future soul mate although complete
May be overbooked

Mothers have good intentions
But must stay in their lanes,
The history of the disrespected black man
Reverses his gains

Like flags flying high at the top of the pole,
The Man of the House must be proudly respected
Even as the strong wind blows

Like the flags, The Man's position should be
Raised and lifted high
By the tender hands of his woman you see.

A boy must respect two men in his life
Or Get out of line!

One is the Great Jehovah,
The deliverer of his future spouse
Two, is the patient one, the one that raised him
To become, "The Man of the House"

"OVERCOME" Words for YOU

Find the Sparkle

The boy refused to work or obey
He hates himself, his life,
So his anger remain in his way

Others look at him and see a worthless pit.
Thats his image in the mirror,
He don't give a blimp.

He wants you to see
A little person in a little place.
Because the lower the expectation
The uglier his race.

He hate the mirror for what it shows
A world where no one cares,
That bad parents control.

Only if his teachers could understand
And tap into that key.
To rescue and inspire the young boy
To be more than he himself can see.

I see his long lashes
Trying to cover his dead lifeless eyes.
But I see more, there it is!
The long lost sparkle
Deeply hiding behind a sty.

I see it, I discovered it, it really excites me.
To discover that sparkle, to find the lost key.

This is why teachers teach,
To search each student to find the key.
To discover the fuel of the student,
To complete thee

Look for and find that student,
Yesterday and today.
An unquinchable thirst, that never goes away

Today it was him,
Tomorrow she will get the share.
The teachers search is endless
Because students need someone to care.

The search starts over tomorrow,

"OVERCOME" Words for YOU

I Like My Nose

Webster dictionary describes
"A Brown Noser"
Suggesting the person is weak.
I'm proud of my Brown Nose
Nothing's weak about me.

Webster then defines "Black-Mail"
Suggesting a dark shady deal,
I'm proud to be a Black Male
The Truth is it's what my Mom instilled.

Webster describes those colorful terms
With such negative disdain
Then why not adopt "white nose"
As the dangerous use of Cocaine

Unfazed by Webster, you don't know me.
It was my ancestor's history and images
We will never forget from tree to tree.

Google your ancestor's, images from
Ireland, England, all over the world...
I look in the darkness of Space,
Of the darkest place,
In a cruel world that continues to twirl

No Google needed, tragic moments to tragedies
Strong images of dogs, fire hoses, and knotted trees

A systematic attack
Design to keep me down,
Webster you don't know me,
You're the clown.

Webster, look in your mirror,
Forgive and forget tragedies past.
I'll remember, and remain proud
My ancestors survived, and were able to last.

As I look into my mirror,
So what! You may not see what I see.
Character-Integrity-Compassion-Honesty

Good noses maybe red at times
Or white, and even sometimes blue
But good noses are
Sometimes brown and even Black too.

Keep your nose clean, don't pick or pry.
Cause a dirty or nosey nose
Make other noses spy

Also, blow your nose softly
As to keep things in order and in place
A nose blown to hard,
Loses its color, shape and space

I confirm my own worth.
I won't let Webster ever define me.
I like my Nose
But more importantly my nose likes me...

"OVERCOME" Words for YOU

<u>My Anger is Mine</u>

**My Anger, my weakness to be,
Because my Dad made a mistake in leaving me**

**He left me! He left me! Damn he wasn't there,
But, my heart forgives him when he comes near.**

**I'm angry; he should have been there for me.
But, when I see him it seems he can make the blind see.**

**I now own the power of anger in my mind.
No-one but me is responsible for my decisions this time.**

**Wow, Wow, a message I can finally share.
I have a great future because I finally began to care.**

⟵―――――――――――⟶

*Are you taking away the attention that others may need?
That's Selfish!*

Magnify Yourself

There is a tool that can manify you.
A closed mind will limit you
A closed mind will limit you from others
A closed mind will limit others from you

An open mind will allow you to explore yourself
An open mind will allow you to explore others
An open mind will allow others to explore you

When you open the Door for Peace…
You close the Door of War…

When you open the Door for Love…
You close the Door of Hate…

When you open the Door for Compassion…
You close the Door of Selfishness…

When you open the Door for Achievment…
You close forever the Door of Failure…

An Open Mind is the tool to magnify YOU…

There is a tool that can manify you.
A closed mind will limit you
A closed mind will limit you from others
A closed mind will limit others from you

An open mind will allow you to explore yourself
An open mind will allow you to explore others
An open mind will allow others to explore you

When you open the Door for Peace…
You close the Door of War…

When you open the Door for Love…
You close the Door of Hate…

When you open the Door for Compassion…
You close the Door of Selfishness…

When you open the Door for Achievment…
You close forever the Door of Failure…

An Open Mind is the tool to magnify YOU…

"OVERCOME" Words for YOU

We Survived...
Today We Rise...

We survived...as a nation deprived...
We cried...as a nation snickered then sighed...
We tried...as a nation conspired...
We abide... as a nation contrived...
We realized... as a nation vilified...
We relied... as a nation seemed implied...
We strived... as a nation connived...
We obliged... as a nation continued to despise...
We revived... as a nation transpired...
We recognized... as a nation refused to visualize...
We ask "Why"... as a nation saw "I"...
We liked "I... as a nation hated the pride of my...
We saw the storm in the sky... as a nation enjoyed the storm and stood by...
We are alive... as a nation mechanized...
We are alive... as a nation continued to hide.
We are alive...because our ancestors survived...
Today We Rise... Today We Rise...Today We Rise...

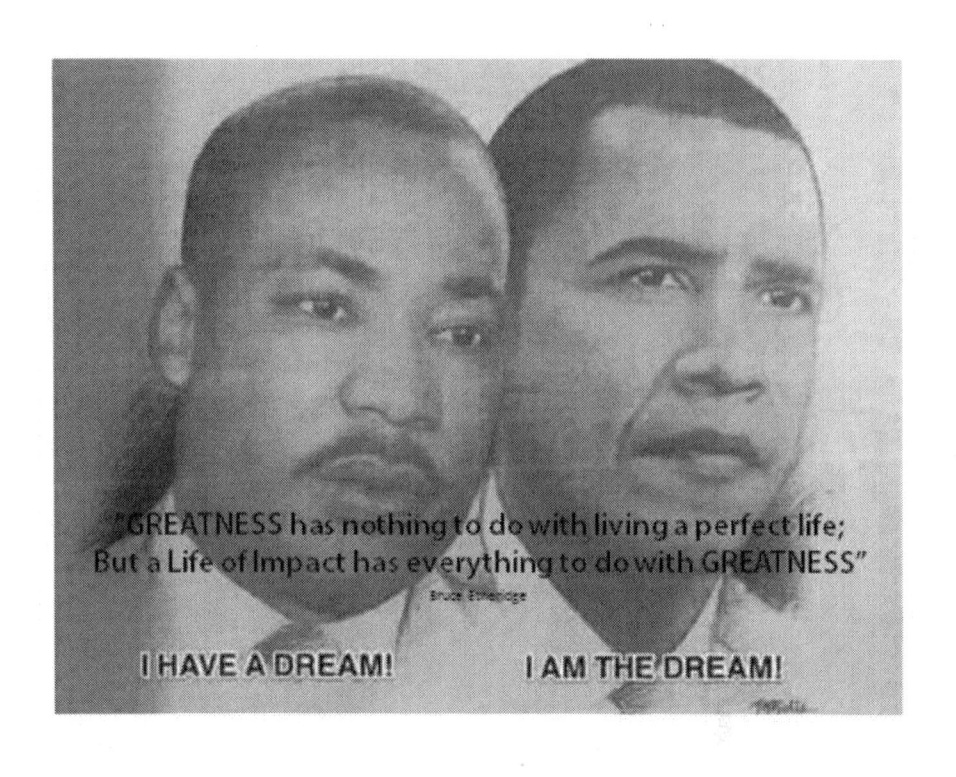

"GREATNESS HAS NOTHING TO DO WITH LIVING A PERFECT LIFE; BUT A LIFE OF IMPACT HAS EVERYTHING TO DO WITH GREATNESS"

Bruce Etheridge

"OVERCOME" Words for YOU

Entrenchment

The Hammer was left hammered...
The Block was sold on the block...
The Pieces was left in pieces...
The Family was hammered, blocked, in pieces,
and left...

Was this the entrenchment of slavery?
Or
Was this the entrenchment of bravery?
We have a choice,
We can be brave for the future...
Or
We can be a slave of the past...

Your focus on crime, just blows my mind,
You may as well tie yourself to the tree.
No patience for the journey of life,
Seeking only the benefits of the destiny.

Partners to the streets, drugs
And crime slowly becomes you.
Pay your bills, especially your rent
Before your family get entreched too.

Were you "Convicted in the Womb" like
"the Brother" said?
Or Convicted in the womb like "the Man"
dreads?

Sail, Cell, Sale anything that not yours,
To make the fast money.
A life so destuctive and fast,
You become the street Dummy.

The entrenched mind of today's new slave
You don't remember the past.
Your mind so entrenched
Due to your own bad weather forecast

Todays new slave see's cloudy skies,
thundersorms and rainy days.
While others see unlimited skies,
a full-time wage while taking care
of family of the entrenched Brave.

Why lead to an old path, for a new slave.
Choose a new path, the path of the Brave

The Hammer was left hammered...

The Block was sold on the block...

The Pieces was left in pieces...

The Family was hammered, blocked, in pieces, and left...

We have a choice...

POLITICS AND THE PRESIDENT

One stood in his way, while the other stood on the side.
The President remained focused with American pride.

The Republicans shut down the Government
The Democrats helped usher American Health Care in,
But during the congressional elections, neither party tried to defend.

Under the Presidents leadership,
The unemployment rate took the biggest Dip.
It wasn't notice because of the Cognac
The Speaker and the House sipped.

The Republican's then complained that
The numbers were flopped.
Training a lie to be their truth,
So the truth would be stopped.

The President and Congress, agree to meet over a drink.
Kentucky Bourbon the drink I think.
The politics of it all continues to stink.

The President pushed for a higher minimum wage,
The Republicans again took at stand.
Against the effort to pay the ordinary Man

Congress represented by wealth and elite
Cash in their hands and Power at their feet
Still no representation for the common Man.
Fighting too hard to stop Yes We Can...

Now we must sit back, wait and see,
Who is stepped on, to meet the elite two percent needs?

The system needs to be over-hauled
Common American values not represented at all!

Thanks Mr. President you played the game well
The fault is a rigged system, and a Congress from Hell.

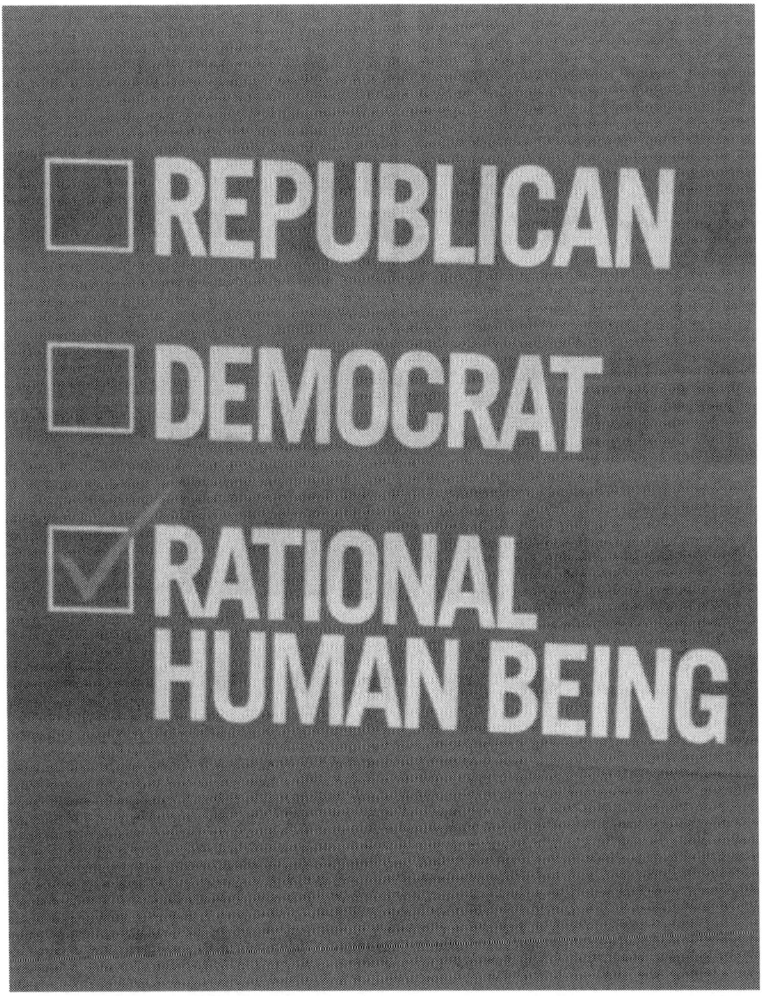
REPUBLICAN
DEMOCRAT
RATIONAL HUMAN BEING

"OVERCOME" Words for YOU

Move On

Okay, I can now clearly see,
The scrowl face that society see in me.
Privileged corruption now our dutiful fight
Blind privilege is difficult to see when the heart feels its right

Blinded by innocence my sight is now clear
I have to overcome the bad odds and their fear
This is not a poem of self promotion or self hate
Its simply meant to help overcome those that discriminate

Inspiring others was my purpose for thee
To stregnthen the roots of my own legacy
Encircled by discrimination, racism, and police brutatlity
While other legacies encircled with corruption but free

The poor and homeless charged a higher fee
To borrow their own money and bank with thee
Hipocracy, Hipocracy is what we see
Then have the adacicity to be my judge and jury

Restricted ability because of a rated credit line
A weighted system design to protect a privileged kind
I don't need your permission to feel what I feel
People need to simply take a stand against the fixed deal

Yet still, we have overcome many intentional bumps
Even though the system gave others a 40 acre jump
Hateful arrogance continue to judge me
The same arrogance that hung precious fruit from the tree

Like a camel, carrying the water of life in it's hump
A heavy load to bear, stick out your chest, I can't slump
Crazy times, killing, women beaten, unarmed men gunned down.
Hopefully good people, common sense, and body cameras will
come around

I also have a dream, my dream and his dream
But the dream I have now is a nightmare it seems
Voter limitation, now their popular theme
Brash, Bold in the open to destroy the Dream

The President and his Office disrespected each day
But he remains cool as a cucumber focus and unswayed
Complaints about his suit color, the color was tan
Is this really about the suit, or the color of his hand

Propaganda its designed to confuse and divide
But the values of Mothers should never be cast aside
Strangers and Politicians will try to tell you what to do
But your grandmothers treasure should never leave you

Stand strong to your convictions, you know what is right
It was engraved in you heart on your birth night
A tough life though, but safe and sound
We got to inspire the youth to American proud

Establish your history, and claim your piece of the pie
Refuse eying others with the sinister sty in your eye
Inspire hope, service of others for generations to come
We can't look back to discover the legacy of a lazy one

A stained legacy stained in my skin color
This stain is mine, a wonderful discover
Our own jugdegment should serve us fine
But take the steps forward to improve all mankind

We, is plural, and should include all
I, is singular, the legacy of I will fall
Young Man, the time has come I hope you hear the call
For change to happen, its all for one and one for all

"OVERCOME" Words for YOU

Raise Your Voice Rise

Raise the level of your People with your voice... Raise your voice to raise your Value... A lost voice is like a lost winning lottery ticket... worthless... Your Voice is Value and Power...

Recognizing injustices and bringing light to them are basic responsibilities of a fair and structured society. Your voice is key to having a quality life. Speak up, speak out, and acknowledge speaking out for truth is not snitching, ignoring the truth or ignoring what is right, is what I call ditching. "The Ditcher" is as low down and can be just as guilty as the perpetrator of wrong... What is done in the dark shall come to LIGHT...

Recognize God favors those that will illuminate someone's darkness to light... With your voice illuminate darkness to light... Let me say that again. ***Always illuminates the devils darkness with God's Light... That is the protection you need... protect your Salvation... Raise and Rise right now...***

The judicial system requires proof *in judgment* **... YOUR salvation requires** *Truth in Judgement* **...**

Speaking against someone's wrong, is fixing something for someone else's RIGHT! The devil is hiding in the mist of your silence **HELLO... message "The devil is hiding in the mist of your silence"**.

"If I die for righteousness, I live forever. If I die with the lie of the devil, I'm tormented forever".

SILENCE is the Devils tool. The TRUTH is Gods tool; it's your Choice… God's watching… God is standing with you in the truth…

REMEMBER

Recognizing and speaking the truth is not snitching. Ignoring the truth or ignoring what is right, is what I call ditching… "The Ditcher" is as negligent just as the actual perpetrator of the wrong in many cases. God sees "The Ditcher of the Truth". If your choice is to protect the Bully, the Thief, the Coward, the Killer, or the abuser with SILENCE, God simply will not allow the "Ditcher of the Truth" into his Kingdom…

As a baby you crawled where you wanted to go, your Mother stopped you…
As you a teen, you walked where you wanted to go, your Mother cautioned you…
As an adult you are running everywhere you want to go…
Pay attention to his stop signs and caution signs…
God is watching you…

Coach Etheridge

"OVERCOME" Words for YOU

"Rerouted Glory"
#30   #10

"Today is not your place of tomorrow"

Well, it's tough to talk about. But Jerode "Smokey" Banks and Cornelious "Weazy" Chiles were simply two over achieving young African American boys from humble upbringings. They both loved their parents very much, especially their mothers. They both just happened to use basketball as a path out. They both had personalities unmatched by any of today's superstars. As I look into the eyes of young people that I teach, I continue to search for the next "Weazy", or the next "Smokey". I search for their character, not their color. I search hoping to find their kindness, their gentleness, their toughness, and most of all their compassion for others.

Smokey and Weazy you see, their impact on me was greater than mine on them. Their impact on us was greater than ours on them. Their loss so tremendous, still today I find it very difficult to talk about. I had a hand in "Weazy's life from his birth until his death.

It's very ironic that both died in tragic car wrecks during the birth of their college careers. The loss of these guys to our community still today is having rippling effect on the youth.

They were difference makers for building character for the lost, they were the difference makers for the forgotten faces walking the sidewalks of low income housing such as "the Manor", or "Crestview" on the eastside of Temple.

They were difference makers for the unfortunate and misunderstood skateboarders that ride the sidewalks of Southside Temple.

They were the heroes to the youth living in the railroad crossing section called "The Vamp".

They were the shining stars for boys and girls living in the section called "The Bottom"

They were the well-dressed prep stars of the future that inspired disappearing racial lines to the North and to the West neighborhoods of Temple.

They taught us to love one another red, black white or brown. They were the best student teachers Temple have ever known. As I see the struggles of my hometown I often wonder what if... What if....What if...

Their story to me has many chapters. It is very difficult because although I had the pleasure to teach, coach, and mentor both of these guys; selfishly I had to come to terms that their purpose had been served. My personal pain, selfishness, and agony for the loss of these two young men should not be misunderstood. I hurt because the lost, forgotten, overlooked, overbooked, and mistook children needed them as

"Hold Models not Role Models".
Our children need someone to hold on to, rather than someone to "Role play and not Stay".
Where are you? Are you a "Hold Model"?
Who are you lifting up?

Are you searching the eyes of those you meet, greet, or teach? Are you turning a blind eye to the needs of others? Have you ask yourself why?

We have eyes to recognize injustice.
We have ears to hear the needy call...
We have a nose to smell the aroma of love, peace and happiness.
We have a mouth to speak up and protect the unheard, the muted, the financially strapped generation locked in poverty.

Those that are beaten down, locked out, due to an entrenched, unfair system designed to keep somebody on the bottom, so someone can feel secure at the top. We still must overcome this treachery. It's very difficult today when we are constantly seeing guys similar to Weazy and Smokey being shot at, or gunned down, choked, provoked, or smoked because of pride. We are dying every day for insane reasons. Let's make this clear, we will no longer accept this, we will demand respect, and we will refuse to be treated as a "BOY"!

As our young men are being choked, shot, and beaten, hearts are being broken along their legs and necks.
All while the two America's live in denial. One America denying their eyes and even refusing to believe in the video while the other America believe their eyes and the video but denying their responsibility to change the pattern. How can we ask young folks to "Shut Up and Get Busy" when the so successful fortunate voices are "Shutting down on their responsibility to get Busy...

"We must stop shutting down and stepping down"
Time has come, for us to be judgmental of others.
Time has come for us to angrily speak of the despair.
Time has come for us to demand justice.
Time has come for us to fix, repair, and for the new America to be fair.
Time has come for us to quit using others misfortunes as a reason not to care.

"Quit building prisons and start building visions"

"OVERCOME" Words for YOU

Stop...Stop...Stop... Stop...Stop...Stop...

*What's up Weazy? What's up Smokey?
What do you think about this?*

I call these young brothers heroes, not to suggest that they were perfect, because they were not. But heroes because of their imperfection, they inspired their coaches, their teammates, their fans, and their home town to believe that there is something greater out there. We must search for the conscientiousness' of those lost along the way. We must find it. We must savior it. We must maintain it. We must capture it, but most of all we must love it and never, ever, lose it.

We have become deaf, blind, and fearful of what I simple call my Grandmother's expectations. The greatest person I ever met........The End...

"Rerouted Glory" #30.....#10

*"I never counted my Wins or Loses,
But I remember every Victory"*

Coach Etheridge

"If you don't live with your Daddy or don't know him... Then it really doesn't matter...

What's important is that you know who YOU are...

YOU can have the biggest influence on YOU...

With the RIGHT ATTITUDE AND MINDSET

"The Real Father Will soon find you"

"OVERCOME" Words for YOU

**'I write my best between the hours of 1am-5am...
...At that time, I'm a better listener of my heart...and my heart is a better speaker to my soul'...**

"My biggest writing fear is not writers block, its running out of ink"

COACHING

Strong character and positive encouragement
He preached to a tee.
Who was this MAN whose name was "COACH"
investing in me?-

Joe Oliver, Carl Pleasant, George DuPree, Leroy Coleman, Don Brownlee, Harry Miller, Vernon Hardin, Richard Herbst, and Bob McQueen,

"Many years of coaching many lives we've turned. The wins and losses not as important,
As the lessons we've learned."

"Coaches that loses games, still qualify for the Championship inside the Gates...
Those that ruin or destroy young lives, may find the Gate Locked"

"To coach or teach is the greatest position I was told.
To coach, to teach, to motivate, a balanced women or man must unfold"

"To the young coaches, getting a new start
Be yourself, do what's right, follow your own,
Not someone else's hardened heart."

I repeat...
We may not always get to see the finished product of our effort. However, the troubled kid will never forget you or what you've done for them...This book is to say thank you and to offer you continued motivation to make a difference.

My purpose is for those reading these pages that you realize help is on the way. Hang in there; just hold on, Survive, Revive, and Thrive...

My goodness, everyone makes mistakes...It's not a life sentence to make a mistake or to be a troubled young kid. Don't be judgmental, crushing, or unforgiving of yourself. You are important, you count, and you are You.
The word INSIGNIFICANT
Should forever be removed from the English Language!!!
Everyone Matters!

"The Greatest Person I ever met was my Mother's Mother"

My Grandmother always said;
"That boy is going to be a preacher or a Pastor someday. He's going lead others to the Light"

She Saw, She Knew, She Believed

"OVERCOME" Words for YOU

Yea… uh hum…Naw Man! **What?**…….*swooooooosh*
The Shoe lands…OUCH… Oh I meant
Yes Ma'am!!!Yes Sir!!!…

Boy, Go get that switch off the Tree"

(Lesson's from my Aunts and Uncles)

RESPECT AT ALL TIMES
Regardless of how old you are

We survived as a nation conspired…
We cried as a nation snickered, then sighed…
We are alive as a nation continues to hide…
We are alive because our ancestors survived…
We are ALIVE…Today we should Rise…   Today we RISE…

How do you want to be remembered?

How do you want to be Remembered?

My Mama's Notes

Ms Lela Etheridge

What makes a Strong Family

1. Godly Parents
2. Be consistent
3. Good listener
4. Discipline not Rejection
5. Parents must love one another
6. Don't play favorites
7.
8. Keep your Promises
9. Pray together
10. Read the Bible together.
11. Have private children devotions

12. Explain How to handle money
    1. save some 2. give some
    3. spend some.
13. tithe ten percent of earnings
14. Discourage criticism
15. Share heartaches Hard times + trials
16. Don't avoid Hard questions
17. Build Biblical convictions into their lives
18. Spend time c children
19. Plan fun things together.
20. Be willing to ask forgiveness.
21. When a problem comes don't take sides
22. always be honest c your children.
23. Be a refuge for one another

The Humane Society of the United States
MEMBER

My Mom gave me this shortly after her 73rd Birthday…it was hidden in her notes sitting in a pile of papers in her office (the coffee table) as she calls it

A Gift for me on her Birthday…

"Nothing else needs to be said"

"OVERCOME" Words for YOU

A Voice From Temple Texas

I awoke this morning thinking of my top 10 personal moments in my life, my top 10 laughs of all time, my top 10 happiest moments of all time, my top 10 most celebrated moments of all time, and my top 10 caring moments of all time.

You came to my mind, congratulations you're in my top 10. Thanks for your efforts. I hope all is well for you. I had a conversation the other day and thought you may need to be reminded this message.

I hope you have your Mom on speed dial... Sometimes mothers make sacrifices that you never know about. Live in the NOW, not in the PAST. Your best days are yet to come. I truly believe that. I still believe that you can become the Man or Women your Mom dreamed of. The one SHE envisioned at your birth. Her sacrifice back then, was for your success today. Life is that simple, we choose to complicate life... Remember life is a challenge, you're not a victim. Also remember;

"You are not responsible for your parents BURDENS. Don't Judge them, fix yourself"

Thank you for the love, the smiles, the jokes, the nice compliments, and the memories. We've been blessed with great memories and great friendships throughout our educational experiences.

I remember laughing more than coaching. To coach you must care first, believe second, and then coach third. Care about others, believe in yourself, and respect all. Don't allow your situation to victimize you. Strive to "Win The Day". If you do that, your life will soon turn around. You will become the Man / Women envisioned at your birth. Serve God's purpose and your situation will change. God will grant you **"Change for a Change"**.

YOU MUST "OVERCOME"

Purchase "Overcome" Selected Poems at
https://www.createspace.com/5320531
also Amazon.com

Purchase "Overcome" Brief and Quotes
https://www.createspace.com/5444133
also Amazon.com

Purchase "Overcome"
Words and Speeches of Impact at
https://www.createspace.com/5470425

By Bruce Etheridge

Copyright 2016 © by Bruce Etheridge

"OVERCOME" Words for YOU

Declaration Page

This book to:_____

I hearby leave this book to:

_____

_____

Dated_____

TO

MY MESSAGE

SIGNATURE

Made in the USA
San Bernardino, CA
24 March 2016